LIFE
WITHOUT FEAR

D1279724

LIFE
WITHOUT FEAR

MIKE FEHLAUER

LIFE WITHOUT FEAR by Mike Fehlauer
Published by Creation House
A part of Strang Communications Company
600 Rinehart Road
Lake Mary, Florida 32746
www.creationhouse.com

Unless otherwise noted, all Scripture quotations are from the
New King James Version of the Bible. Copyright © 1979,
1980, 1982 by Thomas Nelson, Inc., publishers.
Used by permission.

Scripture quotations marked KJV are from the King James
Version of the Bible.

Scripture quotations marked AMP are from the Amplified
Bible. Old Testament copyright © 1965, 1987 by the
Zondervan Corporation. The Amplied New Testament
copyright © 1954, 1958, 1987 by the Lockman Foundation.
Used by permission.

Scripture quotations marked NIV are from the Holy Bible,
New International Version. Copyright © 1973, 1978, 1984,
International Bible Society. Used by permission.

Library of Congress Catalog Card Number: 00-102008
International Standard Book Number: 0-88419-672-0

0 1 2 3 4 5 6 7 VERSA 8 7 6 5 4 3 2 1
Printed in the United States of America

*I want to dedicate
this book to all those who have
experienced the effects of fear. Whether
you suffer the paralyzing terror of a phobia
or the nagging, subtle expressions of worry
and anxiety. Whether you are a young mom,
a hard-working dad, a preacher or a
businessman. Anyone who desires to serve
God with the fullest liberty, this book
is for you. I trust that in the pages of this
book you find the freedom that Jesus
purchased for you through His
finished work.*

I want to thank my wife, Bonnie, for being willing to put our family schedule "on hold" while I wrote this manuscript. Bonnie, you are such a source of life and encouragement to me. I understand when the Scriptures say that when a man finds a wife, he finds a good thing and obtains favor with the Lord. I certainly have.

I also want to thank the partners of Foundation Ministries for their support and prayers. Thank you all for helping Bonnie and me carry God's message of hope and love to the world.

I want to thank our friends who have demonstrated so clearly how much they believe in Bonnie and me and in what we are doing: Andrew and Jamie Wommack, Lee Grady, Stephen and Joy Strang, the guys at East Coast (you know who you are), my parents and family, Pastor Ted Haggard, Joseph Thompson and the rest of the staff and church family at New Life Church, as well as all our friends in ministry throughout the country. You are all a great blessing!

Contents

Chapter 1

FEAR—
MAN'S FIRST ENEMY

The screams gradually became clearer until suddenly Karen awoke with a start from the cloudiness of a deep sleep. She raced toward the room of her six-year-old son, Jonathan. Turning on the light she found Jonathan sitting up in his bed and screaming in a state of sheer terror. She quickly grabbed him, held him close to her chest, kissed his forehead and rocked back and forth until Jonathan's screams subsided. "What's the matter? Did you have a nightmare, Sweetheart?"

"I don't remember, Mom. I don't know what I was dreaming about. I jus' woke up and I was screaming," Jonathan answered.

Jonathan's inexplicable middle-of-the-night outbursts

of fear continued for several months. Karen took Jonathan to the doctor. She even took him to see a counselor. No one was able to explain what was causing his night terrors.

Thirty years have passed, and Jonathan's tormenting nights are just a faint memory. He no longer wakes up screaming in the middle of the night. But he is aware that fear has always been a large part of his life. Recently he became more aware of how the fear of rejection has caused him to sabotage his relationships—especially his relationships with women. After all, he is thirty-six years old and still single! Jonathan is also now aware of the subtle attitudes of fear that have affected his work. His lack of self-confidence concerning his responsibilities at the office has caught the attention of his boss. Jonathan is sure that it is just a matter of time until he is fired from his job for the second time this year.

Nothing is more paralyzing than the emotion of fear. I believe that fear plays a larger part in our lives and in our decisions than we realize. Yet, we seem to have a love/hate relationship with this powerful emotion. In certain settings we enjoy the exhilarating rush of fear—such as the thrill of a ride on a roller coaster at an amusement park. I remember when Bonnie and I took our children several years ago to MGM Studios in Orlando. Janae and Josiah couldn't wait to ride the Tower of Terror, a new attraction at the park. We stepped into an elevator-like compartment and slowly ascended several stories. After a slight pause at the top, the elevator dropped hundreds of feet at sixty miles per hour. They loved it! I hated it! Even though I knew the ride would suddenly drop at extreme speeds, I still experienced a degree of fear (for me it really was terror).

Some of the highest money-grossing movies in the summer of 1999 were films designed to leave the viewer on the edge of the seat, gripped with fear or anticipation. The movie *The Sixth Sense* grossed $29.3 million in its first week of release. The surprise sleeper, *The Blair Witch Project*, grossed $4.1 million its first week at the box office and cost only $40,000 to produce. No doubt about it, in controlled situations we like to be frightened.

Yet I've heard of people who saw *The Blair Witch Project* and discovered that the fear they invited into their hearts in the theater wasn't so easy to leave behind at the end of the movie. Many individuals had difficulty shaking the fear that something horrible might happen to them. Many even awakened, like Jonathan, in the middle of the night in a cold sweat of terror. These kinds of situations feed our hearts with fear and, depending on the individual, can literally take over our lives.

A SOCIETY MARKED BY FEAR

We live in an age dominated by fear. Each year we spend billions of dollars on elaborate security systems for our cars, homes and offices. The power of the emotion of fear ranges from a subtle undercurrent of worry to intense feelings of panic that imprison people in their own personal phobias. When unreasonable fears become serious enough to interfere with our daily lives, they are called *phobias*.

The Institute for Mental Health estimates that over 12 percent of the population—more than twenty-three million Americans—suffer from anxiety disorders. The fifth most common complaint made to medical doctors and psychotherapists relates to severe bouts with some form of anxiety. Each year thirty million or more new prescriptions are filled for medications to treat anxiety disorders.

It is estimated that 5 percent of Americans suffer from some type of phobia that requires treatment. What is the definition of a phobia? A *phobia* is "an intense, unrealistic fear of an object, event or a feeling." According to the Institute for Mental Health, there are three basic types of phobias.

There are *simple* phobias—intense fears that include fear of death, cancer, insanity, the devil, enclosed places, the dark, flying, storms, insects, dogs and others.

For example, for five years one doctor of medicine and psychiatry refused to use a personal computer. He couldn't even find the courage to touch one. He was an author, and his fear required that he type his manuscript using a typewriter. Then his wife would enter it into the computer. When asked about his fear, the doctor responded by saying, "All I knew was that I was uncomfortable near a computer. My fears weren't specific. They were inchoate, irrational."

One Seattle resident suffered from an all-consuming fear of spiders. To avoid the possibility of being confronted by a spider, she sealed her bedroom windows with duct tape. She sprayed her car with bug killer and kept every single piece of clothing in its own sealed plastic bag.

Another woman was so afraid of spiders that when she thought she felt one in her bed one night, she insisted her husband take the bed completely apart until he found it. One day long after that incident, a spider fell from her sun visor while she was driving, nearly causing her to wreck her car. It was then she decided to seek treatment.

Another simple phobia is the fear of flying. Some time ago, I read an article by one journalist who described her fear of flying and how she confronted it. She joined seventy-two other individuals, who also suffered with the fear of flying, for a short flight to the Cherbourg peninsula and back. She described how some passengers boarded the plane in tears of distress and anguish. Others had to be coaxed on the aircraft by staff and crew. Some had not been on a plane in thirty years. Others flew only after consuming a measure of alcohol, taken with drugs like Valium. One lady had booked a flight for a future holiday getaway with her children and had been crying every day since she bought the tickets five weeks earlier.

Another type of phobia is *social phobias*, which include the fear of speaking publicly, meeting people, crowds and crowded places. One man hated to go to work on days when there would be meetings where he and his coworkers discussed current projects. Many times he couldn't sleep the night before in anticipation—or fear—of the next day's meeting. When it was his turn to speak, he would stammer and stutter, his face would turn red and he would struggle to remember what he was supposed to say.

A third type of phobia is *agoraphobia*, a fear of being helpless in an embarrassing or inescapable situation that is characterized by the avoidance of open or public places like a mall or a movie theater. People with this phobia are often trapped in their homes, refusing to go outside for fear of some unknown horrible thing happening to them. The symptoms of a phobic attack are feelings of extreme panic accompanied by a rapid heart rate, sweaty palms, numbness in the extremities, rapid breathing and even disorientation.

One summer weekend day on the upper level of the George Washington Bridge, an incident of agoraphobia occurred. A woman in her early thirties had pulled her car over to the far right side of the toll supervisor's area on the New Jersey side of the bridge. She was convinced that the bridge couldn't possibly hold the weight of all the cars traveling on it and would collapse. No matter how much the toll supervisor encouraged her by explaining the integrity of the structure of the bridge, she would not drive her car over the bridge. It was two hours later that she finally made her way across the bridge.

Jerilyn Ross describes her first phobia attack. She was twenty-five years of age and was touring Europe with a friend. Jerilyn found herself enjoying a candlelit dinner at a mountainside cafe in Austria. She had just gotten on the dance floor and had begun to waltz with a handsome stranger. The floor-to-ceiling windows in the cafe offered a panoramic view of the mountains with the glittering lights of the city below. That's when it happened. Suddenly, Jerilyn felt an overwhelming impulse to fling herself toward the windows. The room began to spin, and she broke out into a cold sweat. She could feel her heart pound, seemingly as if it would eventually force itself right out of her chest. For several minutes of sheer terror, she feared that she might fling herself through the window and onto the cliffs below. Somehow she made it back to the hotel and to her room. From that time on, Ross lived imprisoned by her fear of heights. She refused social invitations from friends who lived in high-rise buildings. She never traveled above the tenth floor of any office building. She felt alone, embarrassed and trapped. No matter where she was, she was constantly aware of this agonizing fear.[1]

Most of these attacks of fear and panic are unexplained. Many times they happen suddenly, without any rhyme or reason. For example, I once read of a flight attendant who experienced a panic attack on her five hundredth flight.

LEARNED FEARS

During the innocence of childhood we find ourselves associating certain emotions to specific situations or objects. These are often derived from events that have happened to us or from words that have been spoken to us by our parents or peers. Even the media can establish how we emotionally respond to certain events or view specific situations.

For example, when, as a small boy, I lived in Florida with my family, we spent nearly every weekend at the beach. I loved swimming in the ocean. I gave little or no thought to what might be swimming with me in the sea. I knew the ocean was abundant with fish life. I remember feeling the occasional bump just under the water's surface, resulting in only a curious response from me. Then I saw the movie *Jaws*.

As I swam all those hours in the ocean, it had never occurred to me that I could be attacked by a shark. After watching that movie, for a long time I was hesitant even to go back in the waters of the Gulf of Mexico. When I did, I found myself constantly looking for that infamous fin breaking the surface and indicating the presence of a man-eating shark. Earlier, my response to the occasional bump of a fish was merely one of curiosity—now it was a reaction of fear and anxiety. This is one example of a learned fear.

An overprotective parent can unwittingly inject fear into the heart of a child by simple warnings like, "Susan, don't go out in the dark; you never know what might be out there," or "Bruce, don't go near the water, or you may drown." Of course, there are appropriate times to warn your children of impending dangers that, in their innocence, they may not be aware of. Looking both ways before they cross the street would be a healthy admonition. So would not talking to strangers and not getting into vehicles with strangers. Warning our children not to touch hot objects is a necessary exhortation. These are examples of healthy warnings.

The important point to remember is that many times fear is a learned response.

Ignorance

Fear can also arise as the result of ignorance. Often, the less we know about something, the greater our level of fear. If our fears are due to ignorance, then knowledge can help us to overcome that fear. Satan takes advantage of our ignorance by "filling in the blanks" with fear-inducing, imagined consequences. Satan's intention is to grip our hearts with fear.

Knowledge will cause fear to loosen its hold on us. For example, those who suffer from a fear of flying often find comfort in a better understanding of the dynamics of flying and of the aircraft's design. Knowledge is a first step to dealing with our fears. Yet, there must be more involved than this. Regardless of how much knowledge you may have about flying—it is still possible for airplanes to crash.

In Luke 21:25–26 Jesus spoke of the powerful effect of fear by saying, "And there will be signs in the sun, in the moon, and in the stars; and on the earth distress of nations, with perplexity, the sea and the waves roaring; *men's hearts failing them from fear* and the expectation of those things which are coming on the earth, for the powers of the heaven will be shaken" (emphasis added).

The medical profession has acknowledged the effect of fear on the human heart. There have been cases where people have literally been "scared to death."

In the second edition of *Mediolegal Investigation of Death—Guidelines for the Application of Pathology to Crime Investigation*, Dr. Werner U. Spitz and Dr. Russell S. Fisher, chief medical examiners of Detroit and the State of Maryland, say:

> [That] an episode of emotional stress, whether it be anger, fear, joy, or apprehension, can precipitate acute failure in persons with organic heart disease, especially of the coronary atherosclerotic type, is common knowledge within the medical profession.[2]

It has been proven that even in people with normal hearts, a sudden release of blood pressure with elevated levels of the hormone epinephrine, caused by an episode of extreme terror, can result in ventricular tachycardia, which is rapid heart action resulting in irregular contractions of the heart muscle that can result in death.

Yet with all of this information, scientists are quick to say that there is much they don't understand about the subject of fear. Admittedly, the best they can do is to offer theories or medications that alter the biochemistry of an individual, thus reducing their fears. But at best, these people go through life medicated; they may rarely experience a complete cure. Only a work of the Spirit of God can truly set us free from fear.

A Spirit of Fear

Where science and the medical profession fail, the Scriptures succeed. Extreme fear is more than a genetic or chemical disorder. It may be that science is able to measure the results of fear, but where it originates is a mystery—at least to the science community. That's because ultimately fear is a spiritual issue.

In 2 Timothy, Paul writes to a young preacher by the name of Timothy. Timothy was one of Paul's disciples, a son in the faith, if you will. Timothy was the pastor of the church in Ephesus. During the time that Timothy was pastoring the church, the persecutions of the Christians by the Roman government had intensified dramatically. Thousands of Christians' lives were being sacrificed for the sake of the gospel. At the same time, others were struggling with the violent fear that they would be next. Like a raging river overrunning its banks, fear was sweeping through the Ephesus church. Even Timothy struggled with a spirit of self-preservation. Paul addressed Timothy's fear by saying:

> For God has not given us a spirit of fear, but of power and of love and of a sound mind.
>
> —2 TIMOTHY 1:7

It is clear from scripture that fear is a spirit—a demonic, spiritual force. It was this spiritual force that had found an entrance into Timothy's heart. Because fear comes from the realm of the demonic, the answer to Timothy's fear would not be found in some form of medication. By calling fear a "spirit," Paul was instructing Timothy concerning the origin of the fear he was battling, and in so doing, he was showing Timothy the cure. And yet, in light of this fact, it is surprising to me that so many Christians address their fears and phobias by placing their trust in the medical profession for providing a solution. Many attempt to conquer their fears through natural resources.

In Paul's letter to the Corinthians, he addresses the issue of dealing with battling spiritual battles by using carnal weapons:

> For though we walk in the flesh, we do not war according to the flesh. For the weapons of our warfare are not carnal but mighty in God for pulling down strongholds.
>
> —2 CORINTHIANS 10:3–4

According to this scripture, we are in a war. Many people, both in and out of the church, struggle with fear that expresses itself in paranoia, panic, depression and even anger. Many struggle with these emotions on a daily basis. Perhaps you do. You may even battle thoughts and feelings of anger, anxiety, depression and fear. Perhaps you can even relate with those previously mentioned who find themselves imprisoned by certain phobias. You may feel as if you have fought your own personal battle with the powerful and destructive emotion of fear only to be left bloodied and defeated.

If we are going to experience victory with this battle, we must realize that the weapons for this warfare are not carnal. Our weapons do not derive their strength from anything earthly. We fight a supernatural battle, and we must fight with supernatural weapons if we are to expect triumph.

As you join with me in this journey through the pages of this book, you will discover a new power from God's Word. Through the divine energy of the Holy Spirit, you will experience a fresh touch of His presence—and live a life without fear!

Chapter 2

MAN WITHOUT FEAR

One of the first recorded words of man, found in Genesis 3:10, states, "I heard Your voice in the garden, and I was *afraid* because I was naked; and I hid myself" (emphasis added).

From the time that Adam and Eve fell in the Garden, fear has been a driving force in man. If we are to understand the negative force of fear, then we need to understand exactly what was involved in the creation of man. And more importantly, we must understand where fear first became a part of man's life. It is as we look at the beginning of man and see the dynamics involved in his creation that we discover the solution to the destructive emotion of fear.

It is in Genesis 2 that we witness this remarkable event.

> And the LORD God formed man of the dust of the ground, and breathed into his nostrils the breath of life; and man became a living being.
>
> —GENESIS 2:7

The first important point to notice in man's creation is the act of God's breathing His life into man. The word *life* in the phrase "breath of life" is the Hebrew word *chay*, a plural word. So this phrase actually reads "breath of lives." The infilling of God produced two aspects of life in man—spiritual life and soulish life. When God's life entered man's body (that which was formed from the dust of the ground), that life created the spirit of man. Likewise, as the spirit of man came into contact with that same body, man became a living soul. From this we can clearly see that man is three parts—spirit, soul and body.

The apostle Paul pointed out these three distinctions of man when he wrote:

> Now may the God of peace Himself sanctify you completely; and may your whole spirit, soul, and body be preserved blameless at the coming of our Lord Jesus Christ.
>
> —1 THESSALONIANS 5:23

THE SPIRIT OF MAN

The first aspect of man at which we must look is *the spirit.* The spirit of man shouldn't be confused with the Spirit of God. It was the Spirit of God that entered Adam's flesh, thus creating his spirit. Because we all find our beginning from Adam, every human being therefore possesses a spirit. For example, in Zechariah 12:1 we read, "Thus says the LORD, who stretches out the heavens, lays the foundation of the earth, and forms the spirit of man within him..." In 1 Corinthians 2:11 the apostle Paul makes reference to the spirit of man by saying, "For what man knows the things of a man except the spirit of the man which is in him?" In Proverbs 25:28 we read, "Whoever has no rule over his own spirit is like a city broken down, without walls."

To help us to further understand the function of the spirit, it is essential to identify two different aspects of the spirit.

Supernatural perception

One area of the spirit is that of *supernatural perception.* Another word for this could be *intuition.* This is the kind of knowledge or "knowing" that comes to us without any help from the intellect. Revelation from the Scriptures or about the operations of the works and gifts of the Spirit are realized through this supernatural perception. This explains why many times we receive revelation from the Word of God and yet find it hard to communicate it to others. We receive revelation by our spirit first. As a result, it takes time for our mind to grasp the same knowledge.

An example of supernatural perception that is separate from our minds can be found in the life of Jesus.

> But immediately, when Jesus perceived in His *spirit*

that they reasoned thus within themselves, He said to them, "Why do you reason about these things in your hearts?"

—MARK 2:8, EMPHASIS ADDED

Another example of the spirit receiving revelation can be found in the life of a man in the Scriptures by the name of Apollos.

> Now a certain Jew named Apollos, born in Alexandria, an eloquent man and mighty in the Scriptures, came to Ephesus. This man had been instructed in the way of the Lord; and being fervent in *spirit*, he spoke and taught accurately the things of the Lord, though he knew only the baptism of John.
>
> —ACTS 18:24–25, EMPHASIS ADDED

According to Scripture, Apollos was preaching and teaching with precision the things of God with little information and no formal training. It was through his spirit that he gained understanding of the things of God. And it was within his spirit that he felt compelled to declare this revelation.

In the Book of Matthew, we see another example of the spirit's ability to grasp spiritual truth apart from the intellect in the life of the apostle Peter:

> When Jesus came into the region of Caesarea Philippi, He asked His disciples, saying, "Who do men say that I, the Son of Man, am?" So they said, "Some say John the Baptist, some Elijah, and others Jeremiah or one of the prophets." He said to them, "But who do you say that I am?" Simon

> Peter answered and said, "You are the Christ, the
> Son of the Living God." Jesus answered and said to
> him, "Blessed are you, Simon Bar-Jonah, for flesh
> and blood has not revealed this to you, but My
> Father who is in heaven."
>
> —MATTHEW 16:13–17

The people in Jesus' time were trying to figure out who He was. It is clear that they were attempting to understand the person and ministry of Jesus strictly from a natural and intellectual point of view. He was being compared to men who had previously lived, prophets and preachers with whom mankind had previous knowledge. Yet, what Peter understood concerning who Jesus was didn't involve knowledge that came from the natural (flesh and blood). According to Jesus, Peter's knowledge was a revelation that came directly from heaven. Peter grasped this truth with his spirit. In much the same way, it was through Adam's created spirit that he was empowered to understand the heart and nature of God.

Intimacy

A second aspect of the spirit is *the ability to worship God.* In the same way that we receive revelation through our spirit, we also discover the place of true intimacy and worship of God. Jesus talked about the subject of worshiping God by saying:

> But the hour is coming, and now is, when the true
> worshipers will worship the Father in spirit and
> truth; for the Father is seeking such to worship

Him. God is Spirit, and those who worship Him
must worship in spirit and truth.

—JOHN 4:23–24

It is only with our spirits that we can worship and
commune with God. Why? God, in His essence, *is*
Spirit. We possess a spirit, but God *is* Spirit. Therefore
He transcends time and space. This is what makes Him
omnipresent. We can direct our souls to Him, placing
our thoughts and affections upon Him, but it is only
with our spirit that we can touch Him in worship and
intimacy.

The following scriptures demonstrate the function of
the human spirit in worship and service to God:

> The Spirit Himself bears witness with our spirit
> that we are children of God, and if children, then
> heirs—heirs of God and joint heirs with Christ, if
> indeed we suffer with Him, that we may also be
> glorified together.
>
> —ROMANS 8:16–17

> For God is my witness, whom I serve with my spirit
> in the gospel of His Son, that without ceasing I
> make mention of you always in my prayers.
>
> —ROMANS 1:9

> But he who is joined to the Lord is one spirit with
> Him.
>
> —1 CORINTHIANS 6:17

THE SOUL

The second aspect of man in his creation is that of the soul.

18

Genesis 2:7 says that man became a "living soul" (KJV). The soul refers to the life of man. A man without a soul cannot live. There are three different words for life in the Scriptures. One is the word *bios*, from which we get our word *biology*. The word *bios* reflects simply the physical life of a person, or it can represent what we would call their livelihood. In the Gospel of Mark Jesus used this word when speaking of a widow who gave into the treasury of the synagogue.

> So He called His disciples to Himself and said to them, "Assuredly, I say to you that this poor widow has put in more than all those who have given to the treasury; for they all put in out of their abundance, but she out of her poverty put in all that she had, her whole livelihood *[bios]*."
> —MARK 12:43–44

Another word for life is the word *zoe*. This refers to the highest kind of life we can experience. It is the life of the Spirit. *Zoe* refers to the principle of God's life expressed in the spirit and soul. When the Scriptures refer to eternal life, the word *zoe* is used to describe this life from above. In the Gospel of Mark we see an example of the use of the word *zoe*:

> Now as He was going out on the road, one came running, knelt before Him, and asked Him, "Good Teacher, what shall I do that I may inherit eternal life *[zoe]*?"
> —MARK 10:17

In another account in the Word of God, this young

man is described as a rich young ruler. This is important additional information. It helps us to understand more accurately this young man's background. With all this young man had obtained in the area of wealth and power, he still felt that he was missing something in his life. There was a dimension of life he had not been able to experience up to this point, and part of him longed for something more. This young ruler recognized that the life he needed was beyond what he had experienced so far. And he knew enough about the things of God to realize that what he needed was eternal life.

The third word for life we find in the Scriptures is the word *soul*. In the Greek language it is the word *psuche*. In the Hebrew language the word for soul is *nephesh*. It is the soul that describes the life of a man or woman. Remember, the soul was produced after the spirit came in touch with the body. The soul therefore is closely related to the creation. It is what defines the life of man—his personality, his thoughts, his will and his emotions.

God's Word often refers to people as "souls." When Jacob and his family journeyed to Egypt, the Book of Genesis says, "All the souls of the house of Jacob, which came into Egypt, were threescore and ten" (Gen. 46:27, KJV).

The idea of the word *soul* describing the life of a man is proved further as Mark records Jesus' words:

> For whoever desires to save his life will lose it, but whoever loses his life for My sake and the gospel's will save it. For what will it profit a man if he gains

the whole world, and loses his own soul? Or what
will a man give in exchange for his soul?
—Mark 8:35–37

The word *life* in this passage is the Greek word *psuche,*
which is translated as the English word for *soul.* The word
soul itself in this passage is also the same Greek word.
Therefore, we see the words *life* and *soul* used inter-
changeably.

In further examination of the soul, we see it is made
up of numerous elements. Some of the dominant elements that we need to look at include the mind, the will
and the emotions. Together, each of these helps to con-
stitute the soul of man. Looking at these elements carefully will help us to understand the function of the soul
and how it relates in the creation of man.

The mind

The first element is the *mind.* One aspect of the mind
involves the intellect. It encompasses the power of
thought. It refers to man's ability to analyze and think
through the issues of life. It is the cognitive part of man,
reflecting his intelligence. There are many scriptures
that describe knowledge in reference to the soul. For
example, in Proverbs 2:10–11 we read, "When wisdom
enters your heart, and knowledge is pleasant to your *soul,*
discretion will preserve you; understanding will keep
you" (emphasis added). In other words, in the same way
that honey is sweet to the taste and delightful to the
senses, so is the wisdom of God to the soul. That insight
and discretion will guide us and protect us in life.

Another verse that deals with the soul's capacity for knowledge is also found in the Book of Proverbs:

> Better is the poor who walks in his integrity than one who is perverse in his lips, and is a fool. Also it is not good for a *soul* to be without knowledge, and he sins who hastens with his feet.
> —PROVERBS 19:1–2, EMPHASIS ADDED

The writer of these verses is telling us that the way to guard the path of our life in character and integrity is to seek the knowledge of God with our soul.

Yet, the mind involves more than just the intelligence. The mind also involves the imagination. *Imagination* is one of the most powerful activities of the mind. Imagination is the ability to think in pictures, which every one of us possesses. The imagination can work in a positive or a negative way. Positively, it was meant to be the part of our soul that enables us to picture the truths of God. When God's Word invades our imagination, true meditation and permanent change take place in our lives.

In Joshua 1:8 we read:

> This Book of the Law shall not depart from your mouth, but you shall meditate in it day and night, that you may observe to do according to all that is written in it. For then you will make your way prosperous, and then you will have good success.

God is charging Joshua to meditate on His Word. As he does, the Word of God will paint a picture in the heart of Joshua of victory, courage, strength and wisdom. That is why God said, "...that you may observe to do..." As Joshua would see or *imagine* the truth of the Word in his heart, he would be empowered to accomplish it.

The will

The second aspect of the soul is *the will*. The will represents that part of us that holds the power of choice. It is our capacity of decision. Being made in the image and likeness of God involves this ability. This is one of the many characteristics that separate us from the animals. Animals operate by instinct. They are only capable of living a reactionary existence. Man is able to choose, to make decisions apart from the influence of his surroundings or environment. We see an example of this when God admonishes Israel regarding their obedience to Him by saying:

> I call heaven and earth as witnesses today against you, that I have set before you life and death, blessing and cursing; therefore *choose* life, that both you and your descendants may live.
> —DEUTERONOMY 30:19, EMPHASIS ADDED

The will is the most sacred part of the soul. Why? Because it is what makes us like God. Yet it is important to understand that God will never extend Himself, or His authority, beyond our will. In other words, God will never force us to serve Him or make us obey Him. He will appeal to us. He will draw us, but He will never force us. If the soul wills to obey God, it will allow the spirit to rule over man as God originally intended. But the soul can also choose to express its will over the will

23

of God, suppressing the power of the spirit. This is a risk that God takes. But it is a risk that is necessary in order to enable us to have a relationship with Him. He wants a relationship with us that is based on our love and desire to serve Him—not one based on our responding as robots preprogrammed for obedience.

Allow me to further illustrate the power of our will. One time as I sat on a plane on my way to a speaking engagement, I began to think about the areas of my life that I knew had not changed over the years. I had heard wonderful messages from the Word of God concerning these areas. With my mind, I completely agreed with what I had heard. At times I was even moved to tears as certain truths of God invaded my heart. Yet despite these responses, I still had not made the changes I needed to make in my life. "Why?" I asked myself. "Where am I missing it?"

That day on the plane I heard the Lord speaking to me concerning the importance of my will. In so doing, He directed my attention to the fourth chapter of Mark, which contains the parable of the sower. (See Mark 4:1–20.) In this parable Jesus describes four different responses our hearts can have toward the Word of God. In verses 16–17 of this chapter Jesus describes one of the four responses:

> These likewise are the ones sown on stony ground who, when they hear the word, immediately receive it with gladness; and they have no root in themselves, and so endure only for a time. Afterward, when tribulation or persecution arises for the word's sake, immediately they stumble.

Here Jesus speaks of those who hear the teaching of the Word of God and "receive it with gladness." These people agree with their minds with what they hear. They are even touched in the realm of their emotions by the truths of God's Word. They grasp the initial concept of truth and become excited, even beginning to run with it. Then persecution and hardship come. Suddenly the very word they were excited about becomes the word that offends them.

In order to better understand what happens with this group of people, we need to look at another group of people whom Jesus mentions in this parable. Jesus describes this group by saying:

> But these are the ones sown on good ground, those who hear the word, accept it, and bear fruit: some thirtyfold, some sixty, and some a hundred.
>
> —MARK 4:20

Initially, the people mentioned in the verses 16–17 look exactly like the ones in the verse 20. It isn't until hardship and persecution come that you can tell the difference. It says that both received the Word of God. But there is a difference in the way they received God's Word. The word *receive* in verse 16 is the Greek word *lambano*, which means "to receive as merely a self-prompted action without necessarily signifying a favorable response." This word describes a passive response. In other words, this person might say, "If this teaching or these truths come at a time of convenience for me and do not require anything of me…then I'll receive them."

A completely different kind of response can be found in

verse 20. The word for *receive* in Mark 4:20 is a different Greek word. It is the Greek word *paradechomai*. The first part of this word, *para*, is translated "beside or along side of." The second part of the word, *dechomai*, is translated "to receive." When combined, this word means "to embrace with an attitude of surrender and obedience that which you are receiving."

The people whom Jesus mentions in Mark 4:20 are displaying another aspect of the soul—their will is involved in their response. The will was not involved with the people in the verse 16. The people in Mark 4:20 are demonstrating the response of people whose will is surrendered to the authority of the Word of God.

It is not enough for us to agree mentally with the truths of God. Nor is it enough to be moved emotionally by these truths. If true change is to take place in our lives, our will must be involved as well. Actually, all three of these aspects of the soul—the mind, the emotions and the will—must be involved for change to take place. And it is clear that it is in the realm of the will that change is established and executed.

Emotions

A third aspect of the soul is *the emotions*. This is the part of us that enables us to feel. It is in this realm of the soul that we experience the healthy emotions of joy, happiness, love, tender-heartedness and compassion. It is also where we experience the destructive emotions of anger, bitterness, hatred, depression and, of course, FEAR. Emotions are what empower thoughts and imagination, positive or negative. It is in the emotional realm that Satan's deceptions find their power. We will explore the different dynamics of the emotions throughout this book, but fear is the emotion we will investigate most fully. At the outset, let me say that the degree of Christian maturity present in an individual is directly proportionate to the amount of control the Spirit has over the emotional realm of the soul.

THE BODY

Once again we look at the pivotal verse in Genesis 2:7, where we read, "And the LORD God formed man of the dust of the ground, and breathed into his nostrils the breath of life; and man became a living soul" (KJV). A vital fact to recognize is that man's flesh came from the earth. The word for *formed* in the Hebrew language is the word *yatsar.* It means "to mold or fashion." This word implies initiation as well as structuring. In other words, God initiated the existence of man, fashioning his flesh as a potter molds a piece of clay.

It is because man's body was made from the elements of the earth that we demonstrate a bent toward the base and unenlightened passions of flesh. The apostle Paul declares this truth in his letter to the church in Rome, saying:

> For I know that in me (that is, in my flesh) nothing good dwells; for to will is present with me, but how to perform what is good I do not find.
>
> —ROMANS 7:18

As long as we are clothed with flesh this will always be true. Temptation will be a part of our lives as long as we are living on this planet. Even Jesus, though He was conceived by the Holy Spirit and possessed the perfect

27

nature of God, was tempted because He had flesh. Hebrews 2:18 tells us, "For in that He Himself has suffered, being tempted, He is able to aid those who are tempted." The Book of Hebrews also speaks of the temptations of Jesus, saying:

> For we do not have a High Priest who cannot sympathize with our weaknesses, but was in all points tempted as we are, yet without sin.
> —HEBREWS 4:15

ADAM'S ORIGINAL STATE

In Adam's original created state, his spirit was sustained by the life of God. He enjoyed unbroken intimacy and fellowship with God. Adam knew God in a way that transcended the intellect. His soul was in tune with his created spirit. Therefore, Adam's thoughts and imagination were captured by the thoughts and imaginations of God's heart. Adam loved the things that God loved, and he hated the things that God hated. Because of this, it was through Adam's spirit that he served God and communed with Him. As a result, in his unfallen state Adam knew nothing of the striving of spirit and flesh that we deal with on a daily basis.

In the next chapter we will see what happened when Adam and Eve chose to disobey God and eat of the tree of the knowledge of good and evil. We will also see the result of that disobedience—discovering when and how fear first entered the heart of man.

Chapter 3

THE SOURCE OF FEAR

I n *the previous* chapter we looked at how man came into existence. We saw that man was made up of three parts: spirit, soul and body. All three were designed to operate with a specific function. The spirit of man was designed to receive revelation from God, then to dictate the desires and will of God to the soul. The soul, then, was assigned to govern the flesh by these very desires. This was the state of Adam after creation, yet this was not the state in which he would stay.

As we discovered in the last chapter, before the Fall the human soul was comprised of the mind, the will and the emotions. The will is the area of the soul where change is established and then executed. Man was created like God in many ways. One important facet of man's creation is the freedom of his will. God has never deprived man of his freedom of choice. God had given Adam the power to evaluate and make his own decisions.

It is important to realize that God will never work His plans in us without our consent. In the same way, neither can the devil work his plans through us without our permission and agreement. God could have made us like robots, placing within us a computer chip programmed to cause us to behave in a certain way. But that was not God's choice. His desire was and always has been for relationship with His creation. God desires a reciprocation of love from us based on His love toward us. God wants us, as an act of our will, to serve and worship Him.

After creating man, God placed him in the Garden of Eden with the task of tending to all the things of the Garden. In Genesis 2:15 we read, "And the LORD God took the man, and put him into the garden of Eden to dress it and to keep it" (KJV). The Hebrew word for *dress* is *abad*, and it means "to work or labor." The Hebrew word for *keep* is *shamar.* This word means "to guard, protect or to watch over." Adam's task was not only to labor within the Garden, but also to watch over it and protect it. His mission was to guard the activity of the Garden, and every part of Adam (spirit, soul and body) was created and equipped by God to accomplish this task

Within the Garden God placed two trees. These two trees would leave Adam and Eve with a choice to make. What they chose would determine the fate of all mankind. Look at Genesis 2:8:

And the LẑRD God planted a garden eastward in Eden; and there he put the man whom he had formed. And out of the ground made the LẑRD God to grow every tree that is pleasant to the sight, and good for food; the tree of life also in the midst of the garden, and the tree of the knowledge of good and evil.

—KJV

Adam had the liberty to eat the fruit of any tree in the Garden, including the tree of life, which God specifically mentioned. But God commanded him not to eat from the tree of the knowledge of good and evil. Even though Adam was commanded not to eat of the tree of the knowledge of good and evil, because of his free will, the choice was ultimately his. He could eat of the tree of life or the tree of the knowledge of good and evil. If Adam had eaten from the tree of life, he would then have partaken of God's nature and life and holiness. He would have lived forever, possessing the very life of God.

The tree of life represents an attitude of surrender to God. It reflects an attitude of dependence upon God for one's very life. The tree of the knowledge of good and evil, we will see, represents an attitude of independence, and to eat of it would be an act of rebellion as well as a declaration of man's independence from God.

Adam and Eve were not alone in the Garden. Someone else had stolen his way through the boundaries of paradise—Satan. And his mission was to destroy mankind.

Satan approached Eve, coming to her in the form of a serpent. This fact is important, because the instruction regarding the two trees was given to Adam. Eve had not been created when God gave His commandment concerning the forbidden tree. As a result, Adam was left to explain to Eve what God had said about the tree of the knowledge of good and evil. This is not meant to be an excuse for Eve's decision, but an insight into the diabolical scheming of Satan. He took advantage of Eve's second-hand information when approaching her. Notice what Satan asks her in Genesis 3:1–5:

> Now the serpent was more cunning than any beast of the field which the LORD God had made. And he said to the woman, "Has God indeed said, 'You shall not eat of every tree of the garden'?" And the woman said to the serpent, "We may eat the fruit of the trees of the garden; but of the fruit of the tree which is in the midst of the garden, God has said, 'You shall not eat it, nor shall you touch it, lest you die.'" Then the serpent said to the woman, "You will not surely die. For God knows that in the day you eat of it your eyes will be opened, and you will be like God, knowing good and evil."

THE PROCESS OF DECEPTION

As we look at Satan's approach, we gain insight into the process of his deception. It has not changed these thousands of years.

Appealing to the soul (intellect)

Satan's first step was to appeal to Eve's soul—specifically to her intellect. Notice again what Satan asks her, "Has

God indeed said, 'You shall not eat of every tree of the garden'?" By asking her this question, he sparked within her a curiosity. Satan knew good and well that God did not say they were forbidden to eat of *every tree* of the Garden. Yet, it was his purpose to engage her in a mental sparring match. This would cause her to lean upon her own intellect, pulling her into the arena of human reasoning. In this way he could pull her out of her trust in the wisdom and safety found within God's Word.

Igniting discontent

The second step in the process of deception was to ignite within Eve a sense of discontentment. Satan convinced Eve that God's reason for commanding that they not eat of the tree of the knowledge of good and evil was because God did not want them to have the same power that He had. Consequently, Satan caused Eve to think that God was holding something back from them. As a result, Eve was no longer content with the life she had enjoyed in the Garden up to this point.

The birth of lust

This led to the next step in the process, which was the birth of lust in Eve's heart. Lust is always the result of discontentment. Lust is more than a sexual drive that leads to immorality. Lust is the attitude that says, "What I have is not enough. I want something more, regardless of the consequences." It can affect every area of life. Just as a river swells, overflowing its banks during flood time, so lust flows out of the discontentment in the heart. Discontentment is like the driving rain, unceasing as it pours itself upon the earth. Lust is the river that arises with each passing moment, until waters overrun the natural boundaries of its banks, leaving in its wake a trail of destruction.

Eve's curiosity and lust blinded her judgment. She felt as if she couldn't stand the pressure of the possibility of knowing more. In Genesis 3:6 we read of her decision:

> So when the woman saw that the tree was good for food, that it was pleasant to the eyes, and a tree desirable to make one wise, she took of its fruit and ate. She also gave to her husband with her, and he ate.

The process of deception is clear. Satan will lead us first through *curiosity*, which then leads to *discontentment*, which in turns leads to *lust*, leading to *sin*, resulting finally in *destruction*.

This birthing of lust appeals to the fleshly desires of mankind. First John 2:16 identifies this lust as "the lust of the flesh." Genesis 3:6 refers to this lust of the flesh when it says that the woman "saw that the tree was good for food."

It is important to see that lust is a strong yet inordinate emotion. It was Eve's flesh that Satan first enticed with the temptation to eat the forbidden fruit. Once Satan engaged her intellect with curiosity, Eve noticed that the fruit was good for food and therefore desirable to the body.

Yet there is a second step to the process of deception within this verse—the lust of the eyes. We find it in 1 John 2:16:

> For all that is in the world—the lust of the flesh, *the*

lust of the eyes, and the pride of life—is not of the Father but is of the world.

—EMPHASIS ADDED

Genesis 3:6 tells us that the fruit was pleasant to Eve's eyes. This is the lust of the eyes. Now two parts of her soul (intellect and emotions) were entrapped by Satan.

If Satan was to be successful in his destructive mission, he would also have to entrap the third part of her soul—and that would be her will. Genesis 3:6 states that the tree of the knowledge of good and evil was "a tree desirable to make one wise." This aspect of Satan's deception correlates to the third step in the process mentioned in 1 John 2:16—"the pride of life." The pride of life is the exertion of *our will* above the *will of God*. This is the essence of sin.

The pride of life also expresses the arrogance of trusting in our own ability, even if it involves our pursuit of God. Often our hunger for more "revelation of God" is accompanied by trust in our own intellect to achieve spiritual knowledge. Therefore, what many find themselves experiencing is a cerebral relationship with God. But as we saw in the last chapter, it is only through our spirit that we truly know God. It is only through our spirit that we can truly worship God.

No part of our soul has the ability to know God deeply. The soul of man was assigned the task of receiving knowledge of God from the spirit. This was God's order. When we receive spiritual knowledge in this way, then our lives are marked by humility and love. When this process is circumvented, then our lives are marked by pride, selfishness and arrogance.

God was not opposed to Adam's and Eve's pursuit of knowledge. He just wanted their pursuit of knowledge to come by His Spirit, which was the process that would lead them to life. Romans 5:12 says, "Therefore, just as through one man sin entered the world, and death through sin, and thus death spread to all men, because all sinned..." How tragic that the path Adam and Eve chose was one of death.

THE EXALTING OF THE SOUL

Let's look again at God's command concerning eating of the tree of the knowledge of good and evil. In Genesis 2:17 God says, "But of the tree of the knowledge of good and evil you shall not eat, for in the day that you eat of it you shall surely die." The Hebrew word for *die* means "to have one executed, to slay, to wither away and decay." This is exactly what happened to Adam and Eve. The moment they disobeyed God and ate of the forbidden fruit, their physical bodies began to decay. It would be many years before their bodies, which were designed for immortality, would cease to function. But more importantly, they died spiritually. Their spiritual death allowed death to have mastery over their physical bodies as well.

Adam's spirit, which before had been alive to God, was now dead. This doesn't mean that his spirit ceased to exist. Every man and woman has a spirit, because we are created in His image and likeness. Because of this fact, everyone will exist in eternity somewhere—either in God's presence (heaven) or apart from His presence (hell).

If we have experienced the new birth, then our spirits are capable of communing and worshiping God. Before the new birth our spirits still exist, but they are incapable of understanding God. The apostle Paul speaks of this fact:

> But the natural man does not receive the things of the Spirit of God, for they are foolishness to him; nor can he know them, because they are spiritually discerned.
>
> —1 Corinthians 2:14

The apostle Paul was saying that a natural man—one who has not received the new birth—cannot understand the things of God. His spirit is dead to the Spirit of God. The things of God are spiritually discerned, meaning that it is only through a born-again spirit that you can understand and know God.

When Adam died spiritually, it meant that the very part of his being that was created by God and that enabled him to know and worship God was now dead. Adam's fellowship with God had been broken through sin. God had not changed; Adam, through sin, had changed.

When Adam and Eve ate of the tree of the knowledge of good and evil, their souls were exalted. Because of their disobedient act, their spirits were now dead, resulting in the lifting of their souls to the place of preeminence. For the first time in their lives, their minds, wills and emotions were left to function without the mastery of their spirits. Their spirits continued to exist, but were now unable to receive and commune with God as they had earlier. Consequently their souls became the governing force in their lives. Without the life of their spirit, their souls therefore were left to interpret everything around them by intellect and emotion.

There was another consequence of their sin, which we can see in Genesis 3:7:

> Then the eyes of both of them were opened, and they knew that they were naked; and they sewed fig leaves together and made themselves coverings.

Adam and Eve became self-conscious immediately. For the first time they noticed they were without clothes. The result of their sin was self-awareness. Adam and Eve had come out from under the provision and protection of God, coming alongside Him in rebellion. Before, their consciousness was of God—they were God-conscious. Adam and Eve's sense of identity was in their Creator. In other words, before the Fall, man's identity was found in the reality and rule of God over his life.

THE CONSCIENCE

As Adam and Eve acquired the knowledge of good and evil, a fourth aspect of their soul that had not existed before was created—the conscience. It was not God's intention for man to have a conscience. Or better put, to have a knowledge of good and evil. When the conscience became a part of man's soul through the acquiring knowledge of good and evil, then it became God's desire to use the conscience to empower man to live in obedience to God.

The conscience is the part of the soul that enables us to distinguish between right and wrong. The conscience gives us the ability to hear the voice of God over the voice of reason. Many times, reason will attempt to justify actions and attitudes that the conscience will judge. But the conscience is not the voice of God—it is the part of our soul that enables us to hear and recognize God's voice.

For example, a transistor radio has the ability to tune into a certain frequency band that enables us to hear the music playing on that particular radio band. It would be erroneous to say that the radio itself is the music we are hearing. The same truth applies to the conscience. The conscience enables us to tune into God's frequency and to be able to determine the difference between good and evil.

THE POWER OF A GOOD CONSCIENCE

Scripture makes several references to the conscience. Each of these scriptures gives a nuance of enlightenment concerning the role of our conscience. First Timothy discloses that there were those in the New Testament church who rejected or put away a good conscience. These people resisted the leading or direction of their conscience.

> ...having faith and a good conscience, which some having rejected, concerning the faith have suffered shipwreck.
> —1 TIMOTHY 1:19

In this example, the result of rejecting a good conscience was that their faith suffered "shipwreck." This refers to the fact that these people's ability to relate to God on a level of intimacy had been hindered because of the condition of their conscience.

It is also possible to injure your conscience to a more severe extent. In chapter 4 of 1 Timothy, the apostle Paul warns about a time when Christians actually will sear their consciences:

> Now the Spirit expressly says that in latter times
> some will depart from the faith, giving heed to
> deceiving spirits and doctrines of demons, speaking
> lies in hypocrisy, having their own conscience
> seared with a hot iron.
>
> —1 Timothy 4:1–2

The word for *sear* is the Greek word *kausteriazo*, which means "to brand in the same way that a cattle rancher, using a hot iron, would brand his livestock." From this Greek word we get our English word *cauterize*, which describes the burning of the flesh, resulting in the hardening or deadening of the nerve endings. Consequently, sensitivity in the area that has been cauterized is lost. This can happen with our conscience. Each time we embrace attitudes or make decisions that ignore the judgments of our conscience, we deaden the sensitivity of our conscience. If this is done over a prolonged period of time, our conscience becomes more and more dull to the voice of righteousness. This results in what the Bible calls a *seared conscience*.

Where does this searing of the conscience begin? It starts when we fail to recognize the importance of holding on to a good conscience by responding in obedience to its judgments. This always begins when we compromise in the small, seemingly insignificant areas of our lives.

Let me share an example of this from my own life. When I first started traveling in 1995, some friends told me that I needed to register as a travel agent. They explained that there would be situations where I would need to pay for my own hotel room or car rental. They informed me of agencies that specifically licensed clergy as travel agents. For a modest annual fee, these agencies would officially register ministers, giving them photo identification cards with an IOTA number. The savings could be as much as 50 percent. Well, initially it sounded like a great idea. So I sent in my annual fee, and in a short time I had my card.

But after a short time of using my card, I began to experience the conviction of the Holy Spirit. Each time I found myself standing at the counter of a car rental company, an agent would ask me if I were indeed a travel agent. I would show my ID card, and the agent would type my IOTA number into the computer. Sure enough, my name popped up as a travel agent. Technically, I *was* a registered travel agent. Yet I was giving the impression that was what I did for a living, when in fact I had no intention of booking any tours.

One time the Holy Spirit even asked me if I wanted to be a travel agent or a preacher. I realized that I was allowing a deception of convenience in my life. Soon after that, I cut up my card. I decided that I would rather pay full price than to reject a good conscience. I knew that if I allowed this deception of convenience in a small area, it would make room for deception in a greater area.

This illustrates the power of the conscience. In 1 Timothy 1:5 we read, "Now the purpose of the commandment is love from a pure heart, *from a good conscience*, and from sincere faith" (emphasis added).

THE BIRTH OF FEAR

The first emotion we see demonstrated by man after the Fall is the emotion of fear. In man's desire to "be like God" and in his pursuit of knowledge apart from God, man found himself not only standing in opposition to God, but also independent of God. Very simply put, man went from being God-conscious to being self-conscious. Along with self-consciousness came a sense of self-preservation. It is within self-preservation that fear resides and incubates until birthed, bringing forth its destruction.

We see this truth in Genesis 3:8–10:

> And they heard the sound of the LORD God walking in the garden in the cool of the day, and Adam and his wife hid themselves from the presence of the LORD God among the trees of the garden. Then the LORD God called to Adam and said to him, "Where are you?" So he said, "I heard Your voice in the garden, and I was afraid because I was naked; and I hid myself."

Adam and Eve heard God's voice, and they ran to hide in shame. Earlier when they heard the voice of God, they ran *to* Him with childlike innocence. But now, the knowledge that they had hungered for had caused them to fear His presence. Why? Because the knowledge they attained came outside of God. It came from disobedience to God. They possessed a knowledge they didn't need—and could not afford to have. This knowledge resulted in a spirit of self-preservation, which created the most primitive emotion known to man—FEAR. They died spiritually and their souls were exalted, causing their emotions to have rule over them.

God responded by saying, "Who told you that you were naked? Have you eaten from the tree of which I commanded you that you should not eat?" (v. 11).

Notice Adam's response in the next verse:

> Then the man said, "The woman whom You gave to be with me, she gave me of the tree, and I ate."
>
> —Genesis 3:12

From his newly birthed sense of self-preservation, Adam attempted to shift the blame both on God and on his wife. Basically, Adam was saying, "My wife is the one who made me eat of this forbidden fruit. It's not my fault. She made me do it. And You're the One who gave her to me."

This attitude is still prevalent in our society today. Sadly, it is just as prevalent in the church. Very few are willing to take responsibility for their own actions. Many Christians want to blame everything and everyone for the condition of their lives. This is the mind-set of a fallen man. This process of thinking has no place in the life of a Christian. And yet, out of fear, most embrace a victim's mentality, convinced they are slaves to their circumstances.

Just as the subtle smell of smoke marks everything it touches with its suffocating odor, so fear permeates and stains every part of our lives with its stench of guilt, shame and despair. What must be clear to us is that fear is a spiritual issue. It came as a result of sin. Therefore the solution is a spiritual one. Fear can and does result in physical and biochemical changes in the body. The results of fear are so documentable, as we have seen, that science is able to measure its effects. But if we believe that the ultimate solution for fear is our own sense of self-preservation, we will never find God's answer to this paralyzing emotion. We will struggle to work our way through our fears, all the while trusting in the resources of man, only to find ourselves still enslaved by our fears. We may even be able to suppress the effects of fear with medication, but we will never discover permanent freedom until we apply the spiritual cure.

I want to encourage you to place your trust in the power of God concerning your fears. Commit yourself to placing your confidence in the ability of His Word to set you free from a life of fear. Expect His Spirit to touch those areas of your soul where fear has imprisoned you. As you look to Him, I know that you will experience His life and peace.

Chapter 4

POSSESSING
YOUR NEW NATURE

I*n the last* chapter we discovered fear's origin and saw that it is a spiritual issue that requires a spiritual cure. It was because of sin that fear took possession of man's soul. Through sin, man's fellowship with God had been broken, reducing his relationship with God to an outward form of worship. Man went from intimacy with God— from knowing Him face to face—to knowing Him only through a system of laws. The reason for this is that man's nature changed when he ate of the forbidden tree, making him spiritually incapable of the deepest communion with his Creator. This fallen nature would be passed down from generation to generation. Genesis 5:3 records this fact, saying:

And Adam lived one hundred and thirty years, and begot a son in his own likeness, after his image, and named him Seth.

Notice that before the Fall Adam was said to be created in the image and likeness of God (Gen. 1:26). After the Fall, Adam and Eve's child was said to be in the image of Adam (Gen. 5:3). That which was lost in the Garden had been replaced by something else. The initial pure nature of man was replaced by the sin nature.

This fact is expressed in man's bent toward rebellion as well as in his struggle to obey God. For example, every child, no matter how cute and precious, expresses this sinful and rebellious nature. Have you noticed that you don't need to teach a child to disobey? Each child does it naturally. In other words, it is their nature.

There is a natural self-centeredness that marks our lives from infancy. Therefore, the Scriptures describe those who are not born again as sinners. Yet, they are sinners not because of what they do but because of *who* they are. It was nothing that Seth did to cause him to partake of his father's sin nature. Adam made a choice to sin. But for every human born since Adam, the fallen nature of man has been passed down to all. The apostle Paul describes our spiritual state before we accept Christ and place our faith in His finished work by saying:

> Among whom also we all once conducted ourselves in the lusts of our flesh, fulfilling the desires of the flesh and of the mind, and were *by nature* children of wrath, just as the others.
> —EPHESIANS 2:3, EMPHASIS ADDED

Notice that the scripture says we lived after the passions of our flesh because it was our nature to do so. Consequently there was nothing man could do to redeem himself. If, since Adam, there was nothing that man did that made him a sinner, then there was nothing he could do to make himself right. Even our acts of benevolence are stained because of this sin nature. We are incapable of establishing our own righteousness. Man needed a Savior.

God prophesied of the coming of this Savior while Adam and Eve were still back in the Garden. In Genesis 3:14–15 we read God's prophetic declaration of man's Redeemer.

> So the LORD God said to the serpent: "Because you have done this, you are cursed more than all cattle, and more than every beast of the field; on your belly you shall go, and you shall eat dust all the days of your life. And I will put enmity between you and the woman, and between your seed and her Seed; He shall bruise your head, and you shall bruise His heel."

From this scripture's description of the Messiah being the "seed" of the woman, it is clear that the Savior would come in the form of a man. In Luke 1:26–35 we read the angel Gabriel's announcement to Mary of Jesus' birth.

> Now in the sixth month the angel Gabriel was sent by God to a city of Galilee named Nazareth, to a virgin betrothed to a man whose name was Joseph, of the house of David. The virgin's name was Mary. And having come in, the angel said to her, "Rejoice,

highly favored one, the Lord is with you; blessed are you among women!"

But when she saw him, she was troubled at his saying, and considered what manner of greeting this was. Then the angel said to her, "Do not be afraid, Mary, for you have found favor with God. And behold, you will conceive in your womb and bring forth a Son, and shall call His name JESUS. He will be great, and will be called the Son of the Highest; and the Lord God will give Him the throne of His father David. And He will reign over the house of Jacob forever, and of His kingdom there will be no end."

Then Mary said to the angel, "How can this be, since I do not know a man?" And the angel answered and said to her, "The Holy Spirit will come upon you, and the power of the Highest will overshadow you; therefore, also, that Holy One who is to be born will be called the Son of God."

The manner in which Jesus came to the earth—being born of a woman—is a crucial point to the message of salvation. The apostle Paul speaks of Jesus, saying:

> Nevertheless death reigned from Adam to Moses, even over those who had not sinned according to the likeness of the transgression of Adam, who is a type of Him who was to come.
>
> —ROMANS 5:14

The apostle Paul is declaring that Adam can be considered a type of Jesus. How? Because the way in which

Adam was brought into existence resembles the way in which Jesus came to the earth.

In Genesis 1:26 we read, "Then God said, 'Let Us make man in Our image, according to Our likeness.'" The word *make* in Hebrew is the word *asah*. It means "to make something from something." In other words, Adam's flesh, his body, was made from the earth, something that was already in existence. Genesis 1:27 states, "So God created man in His own image; in the image of God He created him; male and female He created them." This verse may seem redundant to the previous one. But the word *created* is different from the word *make* that we saw in verse 26. The Hebrew word for *created* is *bara*. This word means "to make something from nothing"—at least not from anything on this earth. Therefore, Adam's flesh came from the earth, but his life came from the breath of God.

Similarly, Jesus' body was formed in the womb of Mary, being made from something of this earth. Yet, as we saw in Luke 1:26–35, Jesus was conceived by the Holy Spirit. Therefore, even though Mary was His mother, His Father was God. This is important, because it was necessary that Jesus bypass the Adamic nature. The sin nature that was passed down from Adam to all mankind was not a part of Jesus' nature. His flesh came from Mary, but His life came from God. Consequently, Jesus was 100 percent man and 100 percent God. For this reason, Jesus is referred to as the "last Adam."

And so it is written, "The first man Adam became a

living being." The last Adam became a life-giving spirit.

—1 CORINTHIANS 15:45

Consequently, Jesus was in a position to succeed where Adam failed. And succeed He did!

THE FINISHED WORK OF CHRIST

Because He had flesh, Jesus experienced temptation just as we do. In Hebrews 4:15 we read, "For we do not have a High Priest who cannot sympathize with our weaknesses, but was in all points tempted as we are, yet without sin." The difference can be seen in the last part of the verse: Jesus was "without sin." Jesus lived for thirty-three years without giving in to temptation for one second. Not for one moment in Jesus' life did He exert His will over the will of the Father. Jesus lived a life of perfect submission to the Father. As a result, He satisfied the perfect law of God, accomplishing what we could never carry out in our humanity. The apostle Paul writes in his letter to the Galatians, saying, "But when the fullness of the time had come, God sent forth His Son, born of a woman, born under the law, to redeem those who were under the law, that we might receive the adoption as sons" (Gal. 4:4–5). In Matthew 5:17, Jesus speaks of His ministry and mission, saying, "Do not think that I came to destroy the Law or the Prophets. I did not come to destroy but to fulfill."

Jesus lived a perfect life, carrying His perfection to the cross. There, through His supreme act of obedience and love, He took upon Himself the sin of all mankind—and its penalty. Second Corinthians 5:21 says, "For He made

Him who knew no sin to be sin for us, that we might become the righteousness of God in Him." As Jesus hung on the cross, He canceled the power of sin and removed its guilt. In His death, He also destroyed the power of death through His resurrection.

> But we see Jesus, who was made a little lower than the angels, for the suffering of death crowned with glory and honor, that He, by the grace of God, might taste death for everyone....Inasmuch then as the children have partaken of flesh and blood, He Himself likewise shared in the same, that through death He might destroy him who had the power of death, that is, the devil, and release those who through fear of death were all their lifetime subject to bondage.
> —HEBREWS 2:9, 14–15

Anyone who places his or her trust in Jesus and in what He accomplished through His death and resurrection can escape eternal death and receive His eternal life. The eternal life Jesus offers cannot be bought or acquired through good works or religious service. It was purchased more than two thousand years ago. It is simply received by faith through the expression of God's grace in the offering of His Son. Paul states this point clearly in his letter to church in Ephesus, saying:

> For by grace you have been saved through faith, and that not of yourselves; it is the gift of God, not of works, lest anyone should boast.
> —EPHESIANS 2:8–9

BORN OF THE SPIRIT

Before an individual receives Jesus as Savior, that person's spirit is dead to God, unable to commune, understand or worship Him. Before salvation is accepted, an individual is governed by the soul and by the dictates of the flesh.

Once we accept Christ as Savior there is a supernatural, divine event that takes place. Our spirit, once dead to God, is quickened at the point of salvation with the life of God by His Holy Spirit. "And you, being dead in your trespasses and the uncircumcision of your flesh, He has made alive together with Him, having forgiven you all trespasses" (Col. 2:13). This is a divine act of God. Salvation is more than switching ideologies and values. It is more than living a moral life. It is supernatural.

Colossians 2:11–12 describes this work of God, saying:

> In Him you were also circumcised with the circumcision made without hands, by putting off the body of the sins of the flesh, by the circumcision of Christ, buried with Him in baptism, in which you were also raised with Him through faith *in the working of God*, who raised Him [Jesus] from the dead.
>
> —EMPHASIS ADDED

It is God who saves us, and His divine work affects our very nature. As a result, we become spiritually alive, capable of knowing and understanding God. Can you remember trying to read the Bible before you were born again, only to find it difficult to understand? But after salvation, when you read the same scriptures again, it was as if a "light" had been turned on, enabling you to understand the essence of their truth. Your spirit, once dead, is now alive to God.

THE TRANSFORMATION OF THE SOUL

Before salvation, our soul had a place of preeminence. Our spirit was spiritually dead. Once we are born again, our spirit is in a position to regain authority over our soul, including our emotions. The Scriptures describe the human spirit, once dead but now alive, as the *new man.* In Colossians we read about the attributes of the new man.

> Do not lie to one another, since you have put off the old man with his deeds, and have put on the new man who is renewed in knowledge according to the image of Him who created him.
>
> —COLOSSIANS 3:9–10

The apostle Paul's counsel about the new man is critically important. Paul's phrase "new man" refers to the spirit of man that once was dead but has been quickened by the Spirit of God. The new man is someone who is now in Christ. Notice how Paul describes the new man: "Who is renewed in knowledge according to the image of Him who created him." This new man is a re-creation by God into God's perfect image. Man's born-again spirit is complete, perfect and whole, just as God is. Kenneth Wuest describes this truth, saying:

> The spiritual man in each believer's heart, like the primal man in the beginning of the world, was created after God's image. The new creation in this respect resembles the first creation. The pronoun

"him" cannot refer to anything else than the new man, the regenerate man. The new birth was a re-creation in God's *(perfect)* image; the subsequent life must be a deepening of this image thus stamped upon man. This putting off the old man and this putting on the new man took place at the moment the Colossian sinner put his faith in Christ.[1]

Notice the last sentence. The putting off of the old man and the putting on of the new man took place the *moment* we placed our faith in Christ. Our born-again spirit was instantly re-created in God's perfect image—pure and holy. Therefore, it is not our spirit that must grow and change, becoming more complete, but rather our soul that changes and is transformed.

Ephesians 4:22–24 makes reference to the new man, saying:

That you put off, concerning your former conduct, the old man which grows corrupt according to the deceitful lusts, and be renewed in the spirit of your mind, and that you put on the new man which was created according to God, in true righteousness and holiness.

The word *new* is the Greek word *kainos.* It does not refer to new as in the aspect of time. It is describing a new point of quality. New in quality as opposed to the quality of the old man, which is marred by sin. The phrase "after God" (KJV) contains the Greek words *kata theos.* A literal translation would be, "According to what God is Himself." In other words, the new man is created after the pattern of what God is in His essence, which is the pattern of true righteousness and holiness.

Thus our new man, our born-again spirit, is created or, better put, re-created after God's image in true righteousness and holiness. Both passages we looked at in Ephesians and Colossians used the phrase "renewing" or "renewed." This obviously refers to a process of transformation. But this process takes place *in reference* to what was accomplished in the born-again spirit. It is a process that takes place within the soul of man—not within his spirit. Many people believe it is the spirit of man that needs to grow and develop. They often substantiate this by quoting verses that contain the word *heart* and show a heart defiled or hardened. For example, in Mark 7:21–22 we read, "For from within, out of the heart of men, proceed evil thoughts, adulteries, fornications, murders, thefts, covetousness, wickedness, deceit, lewdness, an evil eye, blasphemy, pride, foolishness."

Many people assume that when these scriptures use the word *heart*, they are referring to the *spirit* of man. Yet, the word for *heart* in the Greek is the word *kardia*. The attributes ascribed to this word are the same attributes of the soul—namely, thoughts, reasonings, understanding, will, judgment, affections, desires, joy, happiness, sadness and *fear*.

It is because of what was accomplished at salvation— our spirits being quickened and re-created in God's likeness—that we are able to "put on the new man," resulting in the transformation of our souls. *It is as we discover the process of putting on the new man that we find victory from being ruled by our emotions, including fear.* The Bible refers to this process as the "renewing of the mind."

> I beseech you therefore, brethren, by the mercies of God, that you present your bodies a living sacrifice, holy, acceptable to God, which is your reasonable service. And do not be conformed to this world, but be transformed by the *renewing of your mind*, that you may prove what is that good and acceptable and perfect will of God.
> —ROMANS 12:1–2

The Greek word for the word *mind* is *nous*. It is defined as "the conscious life of a man." The mind contains a man's thoughts, desires and his power of choice. It refers to more than just the intellect; it refers to the entirety of a man's soul.

MEDITATION, REVELATION, TRANSFORMATION

By meditating on the Word of God we experience the renewing of the mind. Psalm 1:2 says, "But his delight is in the law of the LORD, and in His law he meditates day and night." The word *meditate* means "to mutter or speak to oneself." It also means "to muse or think." The common Eastern religious concept of meditation is to empty one's mind of conscious thought. In contrast, the biblical idea of meditation is just the opposite. The biblical idea of meditation is to fill the mind with conscious thoughts of God's Word. As we allow the Word of God to invade our conscious thought, we are able to renew our minds. This results in the release of the new life of the Spirit. *The more our minds are trans-*

formed by the Word of God, the more authority our spirit has over our soul, which includes our thoughts and emotions. Look at Hebrews 4:12:

> For the word of God is living and powerful, and sharper than any two-edged sword, piercing even to the division of soul and spirit, and of the joints and marrow, and is a discerner of the thoughts and intent of the heart.

The Word of God is living and powerful. The Scriptures carry the breathings of God. It was God's breath that caused Adam to become a living soul. God's breath created life in Adam. Likewise, it was the breath of the Spirit that inspired men to write the Scriptures.

> All Scripture is given by inspiration of God, and is profitable for doctrine, for reproof, for correction, for instruction in righteousness, that the man of God may be complete, thoroughly equipped for every good work.
>
> —2 TIMOTHY 3:16

In the Amplified translation, the phrase "given by inspiration of God" is translated "God-breathed." The Word of God is more than just a manual for living. It is more than black and red words on white paper. It is a supernatural book! Jesus said of His words in John 6:63: "It is the Spirit who gives life; the flesh profits nothing. The words that I speak are spirit, and they are life."

There is a dynamic relationship between the work of the Spirit and the Word of God. It is at the point where these two elements converge that true meditation takes place. Jesus speaks of the results of the Holy Spirit's inter-action with the Word of God in Mark 4:21–22, saying:

> Is a lamp brought to be put under a basket or under a bed? Is it not to be set on a lampstand? For there is nothing hidden which will not be revealed, nor has anything been kept secret but that it should come to light.

The lamp refers to the *work* of the Holy Spirit in our lives, and the lampstand refers to the *place* of God's Word in our lives. There are many Christians to whom I would refer as "lamp people." They love the things of the Spirit and the gifts of the Spirit. They love to flow in the Spirit. Yet they have no foundation in the Word of God. Because of their lack of foundational knowledge of God's Word, at times they may err by interceding for things contrary to God's written will or by hanging on to "revelations" they are unwilling to abandon, even when these revelations are contrary to Scripture.

Some of these people have grand visions and dreams concerning the kingdom, but they continue to suffer one defeat after another in their personal lives. Often their lives are marked by emotional ups and downs. What and how they feel is the standard they use to interpret the events around them. Their emotional roller-coaster ride brings them extreme times of jubilation, followed by similar times of depression and anxiety with the same intensity. They are double-minded and unstable in all their ways, unpredictable and unreliable. They are con-stantly chasing the latest trend and jumping on the next "band wagon" in the body of Christ. They are lamps without a lampstand.

In contrast, there are people to whom I refer as "lampstand people." They love to study the Bible. They enjoy spending hours in Greek word studies, poring over their lexicons and concordances. Don't misunderstand me; there is nothing wrong with studying the Scriptures in this way. But lampstand people have a cerebral approach to the Scriptures. They rely on the power of their intellect to interpret the Word of God. If you were to caricature them, they would look a little chihuahua dog with a big German shepherd head. Their intellect has been over-developed. Instead of searching the Scriptures and allowing the Holy Spirit to breathe the Word upon them to bring revelation, they humanly reason their way through the Bible. Therefore, like a lampstand, they are bolted into the wall, inflexible and immovable. The Holy Spirit could break loose in a service with miracles, and these people would be trying to figure out what happened.

Jesus wants us to do more than avoid either extreme. He wants us to understand both the work of the Spirit and the Word of God in our lives. This relationship is imperative if we are to experience His power over our souls. Look at what Jesus said would be the result of this dynamic relationship between the Word and the Spirit.

> For there is nothing hidden which will not be revealed, nor has anything been kept secret but that it should come to light.
>
> —MARK 4:22

What are those things hidden that will be revealed?

59

What are those things that have been kept secret that are now known? Well, they are not secrets to God. He knows all things. Rather, they are secrets to us. They are the hidden things in our souls that we are not aware of that have placed a ceiling in our hearts keeping God's power from being released in our lives. We many times refer to them as personal blind spots that trip us up time and time again. For example, the young lady who has five different times found herself marrying the same man. He may have a different last name. He may be a different person, but he is the same kind of guy, abusive and unfaithful. When the relationship between the Word and the Spirit, through meditation, is engaged, then this precious young lady begins to realize what it is in her soul that causes her to be attracted to the abusive man. Once she knows what that is, she then is in the position to renew her mind in that area, breaking the destructive cycle of abuse.

As we saw earlier, the writer of the Book of Hebrews describes the Word of God as a two-edged sword that pierces the heart of man to the point of the division of soul and spirit. Notice, it doesn't say that the Word divides the soul from the spirit. But rather, it brings the division of the soul *and* spirit. In other words, the Word of God is the only spiritual force that has the ability to distinguish between the activities of the soul and those of the spirit. It goes on to say in Hebrews 4:12 that as a result of this division, we are able to discern the thoughts and intentions of the heart. This is why the apostle Paul said that it is through the renewing of the mind that we are transformed so that we are able to discern the perfect will of God.

It is as we apply the Word of God, through the work of the Spirit, to our lives that the living Word is able to help us distinguish whether we are living by the power of our souls or by the power of the Spirit. If we find ourselves being ruled by a strong emotion like fear, for example, then the Word has the ability to divide in our minds between the spirit and the soul, allowing the spirit to exercise its authority over the soul (our emotions). If, for example, we are angry over something, then the division of soul and spirit by the Word will help us to recognize if our anger is righteous indignation (of the spirit) or selfishly motivated (of the soul). This is a lifelong and daily process called the renewing of the mind. The more we surrender our soul to authority of the Word, the easier it becomes to make the distinction between soul and spirit. Eventually, our level of discernment becomes clearer and more accurate, and it is with more ease that we are able to detect the motives of our heart.

Chapter 5

BURNING THE
FUSE OF ANGER

O*n April 20,* 1999, the entire country seemed to gasp in horror collectively as news of the Columbine High School shootings rapidly spread through the media like a dry grass fire. Bonnie and I had just finished lunch at Pizza Hut with some friends. We were in the car and on our way to pick up our son, Josiah, from school. The regular radio programming was interrupted by the news flash. Littleton is about forty-five minutes from our home in Colorado Springs. As Josiah came out to the car, it was obvious that he had already heard the news.

We prayed.

And along with the rest of the world, we waited—waited to hear what would happen next.

As we all would later discover, two students of Columbine High School, Eric Harris and Dylan Klebod, entered the school wearing black trench coats and carrying automatic weapons. Once the carnage was over, fourteen students and one teacher lay dead as Columbine was baptized in a crimson pool of anger and hatred. In the May 3 edition of *Time* magazine, in an article titled "The Littleton Massacre," Nancy Gibbs writes:

> The story of the slaughter at Columbine High School opened a sad national conversation about what turned two boys' souls into poison. It promises to be a long, hard talk, in public and in private, about why smart, privileged kids rot inside. Do we blame the parents, blame the savage music they listen to, blame the ease of stockpiling an arsenal, blame the chemistry of cruelty and cliques that has always been a part of high school life, but has never been so deadly? Among the many things that did not survive the week was the hymn that all parents unconsciously sing as they send their children out in the morning, past the headlines, to their schools: "It can't happen here, Lord, no, it could never happen here."[1]

What happened at Columbine is a stark example of the fierce emotions of both anger and fear. It was anger, fueled by pure evil that possessed the hearts of Harris and Klebold. And now it is fear that paralyzes both parents and children. Long after the ink has faded on the startling headlines, there is the horrific aftermath. Cassie Bernall was one of the students killed at

Columbine. She was shot after allegedly affirming her faith in God. In sharing about her daughter and the aftereffects of the shooting in her book, *She Said Yes*, Misty Bernall, Cassie's mother, writes:

> One thing that's been helpful to me in getting over everything is reminding myself that I am not the only one who is suffering, and trying to reach out to others who are struggling like I am. One survivor from the library, an athlete who was always a fairly confident young man, is still visibly shaken, though it's been over a month since the shooting. He is unable to look strangers in the eye and nervously picks at his hands when he speaks. Then there is the boy from the neighboring subdivision, a strapping sixteen-year-old who doesn't even attend Columbine, who has been having nightmares, including one in which two gunmen came into his room and sat on the edge of his bed. According to the local paper, some girls in the area have so much trouble at night that they ask their mothers to sleep with them.[2]

The first time we see fear in the Scriptures is when Adam, out of fear, hid himself when he heard the voice of God. Thus this birthing of fear affected the way in which Adam related to God. Shortly after Adam's fear response, another powerful yet damaging emotion is expressed by mankind. This emotion is one that affects how man relates to others. It is *anger*:

Cain and Abel were the offspring of Adam and Eve. They both had an opportunity to learn from their father,

Adam, the acceptable form of worship that God had instituted after the Fall. Yet Cain decided to worship God on his own terms, ignoring God's instructions. Abel, on the other hand, obeyed the commands of God and worshiped accordingly. In Scripture we see that as a result, Abel's offering was acceptable to God, but Cain's was not.

> Now Adam knew Eve his wife, and she conceived and bore Cain, and said, "I have acquired a man from the LORD." Then she bore again, this time his brother Abel. Now Abel was a keeper of the sheep, but Cain was a tiller of the ground. And in the process of time it came to pass that Cain brought an offering of the fruit of the ground to the LORD. Abel also brought of the firstborn of his flock and of their fat. And the LORD respected Abel and his offering, but He did not respect Cain and his offering. And Cain was very angry, and his countenance fell.
>
> —GENESIS 4:1–5

The root of the word *anger* (*wroth* in the King James Version) in the Hebrew language means "to burn." The idea behind the entire word means "to burn with anger or to be incensed." As Cain's anger continued to grow, it finally resulted in the first act of murder by man.

> Now Cain talked with Abel his brother; and it came to pass, when they were in the field, that Cain rose up against Abel his brother and killed him.
>
> —GENESIS 4:8

The first emotion we see after the Fall of man is fear.

66

Burning the Fuse of Anger

The second negative emotion we see in the Scriptures is anger. I believe that it is more than coincidence that we see these two destructive emotions mentioned side by side. I am convinced that there is a powerful relationship between the two. They feed off one another, working hand in hand to enslave men in hatred and jealousy.

A SOCIETY MARKED BY ANGER

More and more, anger has made an indelible mark on our society. It is estimated that by the time a ten-year-old child today reaches eighteen years of age, that child will have seen from media over two hundred thousand acts of violence and forty thousand murders.

One troubling example is the world of professional wrestling. Professional wrestling has evolved from the simple entertainment of the fifties to the bizarre and bloody exhibition of the nineties. Teenage boys are setting up neighborhood wrestling matches where they imitate their heroes of the ring. But there's a big difference—these teens are throwing each other into real barb-wired fences. They are smashing each other with real chairs. And when they bleed, unlike their professional counterparts, they bleed real blood.

The increasing problem of road rage is another example of how the spirit of anger is affecting our society. Approximately forty thousand deaths every year are attributed to road rage. Along with the deaths, six million crashes, three million serious injuries and two hundred billion dollars in annual costs result.[3] In Dallas, Texas, a former financial analyst was sentenced to death after testifying that road rage led him to shoot and kill two truck drivers. Douglas Alan Feldman opened fire on truck driver Robert Everett in August of 1998. Everett, thirty-six years of age, was murdered on U.S. 75 north of Dallas. Feldman's rage erupted when he became convinced that Everett almost ran him over as he rode his motorcycle near Everett's truck. Nicolas Valasquez, sixty-two years of age and also a truck driver, angered Feldman, too. Forty minutes after the first shooting incident, Valasquez was shot and killed by Feldman at a Dallas gasoline station.[4]

In our quaint city of Colorado Springs, a man is now standing trial for the death of his wife, a popular disc jockey on one of our local radio stations. A neighbor testified that she heard a scream around 8:00 A.M. on August 29, 1999. The neighbor looked out her window and saw the husband of the disc jockey on the front lawn, sitting on his wife's chest as he choked her. The neighbor said that the wife's "vigorous kicking slowly subsided and then finally stopped." The neighbor went on to say that the man kept his hands on his wife's neck for nearly a minute longer before sliding off her, nudging her and then walking back into his home. The husband was later arrested and tried for second-degree murder.[5]

These are obviously extreme examples of the destructive results of anger. Yet I am convinced that the damaging effects of this emotion are not limited to those "in the world." Behind the sacred walls of the church are many who silently, and in shame, struggle with a spirit of anger, as well as those who are anger's victims. It may be a husband who, in a heated argument, punctuates his point with a backhand to his wife. Or a mother who, out of exasperation, goes several steps too far when disciplining her strong-willed child.

A spirit of anger is demonstrated not only by obvious outbursts. There are other ways that anger is demonstrated. Some of these ways are briefly stated below.

The slow burn

There is an anger that I call the "slow burn." This is where someone is deeply angry, yet silently fumes over an injustice for years before expressing their rage, much like a dormant volcano just waiting to erupt. On August 5, Mark Barton walked into the Atlanta office of Alltech Investment Group. As Mr. Barton casually conversed with the manager and secretary of the investment firm, they both greeted Mark by name. They knew him as one of their regular day traders.

What they didn't know was that Mark was carrying a 9-mm Glock and a 45-caliber Colt. They also didn't know that on Tuesday, Barton had killed his wife. On Wednesday he had murdered his son and daughter. Moments before he walked into their office, he had been across the street at Momentum Securities, opening fire and killing four people. The sound of five shots rang out, and the secretary and manager lay on the floor seriously wounded. Barton went up the stairs to the trading floor where he continued his fury. Five people died at the Alltech office.

As the police cornered Barton at a gas station in an Atlanta suburb, Barton turned the Glock on himself. When friends and associates were asked about Barton, they all related the same thing. He was a likable man. It appeared that he had a healthy relationship with his wife and children. But Barton had been suffering large financial setbacks as a result of some bad investments. Mark Barton hid his anger and rage from others for years before exploding in a murderous rampage.[6]

This is an excessive instance of deep-seated anger that eventually boils to the point of eruption. Most of the people who deal daily with the slow burn of anger express their anger through a general angry approach to life. They are quick-tempered, exploding over the general frustrations of life. They may rehearse an offense in their minds for months until an entirely separate situation "sets them off," often taking their friends or loved ones completely by surprise.

A spirit of rebellion

Rebellion is often an expression of anger. Many times a teenager who seems to find every opportunity to buck against the system in school and at home is a teenager who feels angry or rejected. These acts of rebellion are attempts to gain the attention that teen feels he or she desperately needs.

A self-destructive lifestyle

Surrendering to a pattern of destructive choices can also be an expression of deep-seated anger. The man who continues to drink, even though his job is in jeopardy from previous warnings concerning his drunkenness, may be a man who is using his self-imposed anger to sabotage his own success. Or a woman who endangers the life of her unborn child with her own continued drug use may be lashing out in anger at herself or at a society she feels has hurt her.

Sarcasm

Sarcasm is also an expression of anger. It is often veiled in humor and verbalized through demeaning or cutting remarks. An attitude of cynicism may accompany the sarcasm.

All of these forms of anger range from simply reducing the health of our lives and relationships to being totally destructive. Neither extreme reflects the glory and reality of God in our lives.

The Scriptures are clear about the destructive results of anger. In Proverbs 29:22 we read, "An angry man stirs up strife, and a furious man abounds in transgression." Within this scripture we see not only how anger affects our relationship with others (an angry man stirring up strife), but how it also affects our relationship with God (a furious man abounding in transgressions).

WHAT THE BIBLE SAYS ABOUT ANGER

There are three types of anger that the Scriptures deal with. We see all three in the apostle Paul's letter to the Ephesians, as well as in his letter to the Colossians.

> Let all bitterness, wrath, anger, clamor, and evil speaking be put away from you, with all malice.
> —EPHESIANS 4:31

> "Be angry, and do not sin": do not let the sun go down on your wrath.
> —EPHESIANS 4:26

71

But now you yourselves are to put off all these: anger, wrath, malice, blasphemy, filthy language out of your mouth.

—COLOSSIANS 3:8

In Ephesians 4:31 the word *anger* is the Greek word *orge*. It refers to anger as a state of mind, a deep-abiding anger that has settled in the heart of a person. Like a river that may look calm but surges with a fierce undertow just below the surface, so is this type of anger. It is like an active volcano, seemingly at rest but filled with hot lava, brooding, boiling, just waiting to explode.

Most of us have experienced times when we sensed intense anger just under the surface of our thoughts and words. No doubt we can recall our frustration as we attempted to fight off our impulses to act on this volatile emotion. When those angry impulses are expressed, we have moved to the next word for anger in verse 31, which is the word *wrath*.

The Greek word for *wrath* is *thumos*. *Thumos* is translated as "a violent motion." It is an expression of *orge*. Another part of the definition for the word *wrath*, further describing its nature, is "to move impetuously." How many times have we found our actions describing that very word? I can recall time after time when I acted foolishly because I allowed my anger to cloud my judgment and perspective. Instead of pausing to put a check on my heart, in my anger I made decisions that I later regretted. Proverbs 14:17 says, "He that is soon angry dealeth foolishly" (KJV). That is exactly how I felt and looked at times—foolish.

Burning the Fuse of Anger

For example, I remember fourteen years ago, just after we started the church in Merritt Island, Florida. It was 1986. I was twenty-seven years old. There was a young couple in our church then that Bonnie and I loved. But even though we loved this couple, a situation arose to cause me to become exasperated with the husband. I felt that his expectations of me as his pastor were unrealistic. Actually, in my mind they were impossible to live up to. Each time I didn't meet his standard, I felt his judgment.

One Saturday as we talked on the phone, I felt that he again, in his own subtle way, had made it clear that I had failed him. In the past I had tucked away each expression of his displeasure in the back of my mind. My anger over what I felt was his unfair judgment of me was buried just under the surface.

I was livid as I hung up the phone. That was it. I had had it. I launched into a discourse to Bonnie about all the times I felt he had held me to a superhuman standard. I expressed that I wasn't going to let anyone "run my life."

As I finished my tantrum, I punctuated my last word with a pop of my fist to the door frame of our bedroom. That's when I heard something snap. I looked down at the outside of my hand, and I saw the impression of a small bone raised to a peak. Quickly I pressed the bone back in place, realizing that I had broken it.

It didn't take me long to realize anew the truth of the Word, which states, "He that is soon angry dealeth foolishly"—or better yet, *stupidly.*

The third word for anger in the Scriptures is found in

Ephesians 4:26. It is also translated in the English as the word *wrath*. But the Greek word is different from the word for wrath in verse 31. The Greek word in verse 26 is *parorgismos*. The first part of the word comes from the root *para*, which means "beside or along side of." This describes an anger that causes one to be beside himself in rage. We use the expression, "He was out of his mind." It is an explosion of emotion that goes beyond *thumos*. It is an uncontrollable rage.

GOOD AND MAD?

Yet with all that we see in the Scriptures about the horrible effects of being angry, Carol Tavris, in her book *Anger—the Misunderstood Emotion*, points out the possible good that can come from anger:

> Most of all, I believe that a careful study of anger matters because anger, like love, has such a potent capacity for good and evil. And I do mean good and evil, not "adjustment and deviance," the gutless language that so often characterizes modern discussions of psychological topics. Anger, like love, is a moral emotion. I have watched people use anger in the name of emotional liberation to erode affection and trust, whittle away their spirits in bitterness and revenge, diminish their dignity in years of spiteful hatred. And I watched with admiration those who use anger to probe for truth, who challenge and change the complacent injustices of life, who take an unpopular position center stage while others say "sshhhh" from the wings.[7]

Burning the Fuse of Anger

There is a word in the Scriptures for godly anger. We are actually commanded to have this kind of anger. In Ephesians 4:26 we read, "Be angry, and do not sin." According to this verse it is possible to have a righteous anger. This word for *anger* in the Greek is also the word *orge*. Yet this is a holy anger. What makes the difference? It is not an anger that is selfishly motivated. It is an anger that deals with the injustices of life. It is a "no-tolerance" attitude for the things that oppose the truth of the gospel.

We have several examples of righteous anger in the Word of God. One is the example of Jesus' driving out the money lenders. We find one account of this event in Mark's Gospel.

> So they came to Jerusalem. Then Jesus went into the temple and began to drive out those who bought and sold in the temple, and overturned the tables of the money changers and the seats of those who sold doves. And He would not allow anyone to carry wares through the temple.
>
> —Mark 11:15–16

There was definitely a strong passion behind His actions. I don't believe that Jesus kindly asked the money lenders to stop their trade. It says that He turned over the tables and refused to allow anyone to carry a vessel through the temple. There was an intensity in Jesus that could not be stopped. Even the Roman soldiers assigned to maintain control over the temple dared not interfere with Jesus' outrage over the abuse of the worshipers in the temple.

What Jesus did was not an out-of-control expression of rage. Jesus had gone to the temple earlier, where He "looked around at all things" (Mark 11:11). Jesus thought long and hard about what He had seen. He took time to decide what His response would be. It wasn't until the next day that He entered the temple to exact the justice of God.

His anger wasn't selfishly motivated, but it was a result of His love for the people and His resentment over how religion had stripped them of their dignity.

Another example of this type of anger is found in Mark 3:5, where we read:

> And when He had looked around at them with anger, being grieved by the hardness of their hearts, He said to the man, "Stretch out your hand."

Once again, we see Jesus' outrage over the Pharisees' love for rules and laws over their love for people and compassion concerning their suffering. This is the kind of anger we are commanded to possess. It is this kind of anger over injustice that has freed slaves, liberated nations and proclaimed the voice of the gospel loud and clear in our world.

Yet, if we are to be able to have the kind of anger that can change our world, we must remove all the damaging expressions of self-centered rage from our lives. In the first part of Ephesians 4:31, the phrase "Let all..." is used. This means all manner or all kinds of anger. It goes on to say that these kinds of anger are to be "put away" from our lives. The phrase "put away" is the Greek word *airo*, which means "to bear away what has been raised, to carry off, to take completely away."

A tremendous amount of damage is done by anger. A tremendous amount of shame comes with anger. There are many who day after day swear that they will never again allow their anger to get the better of them, only to suffer another painful defeat.

WHAT MAKES US ANGRY?

Part of the problem is that we usually deal with anger as a separate emotion. If we don't discover the root of anger, we will never find freedom from its destructive forces. To begin to discover the root of anger, we need to understand what makes us angry.

There are basically two reasons why anger gets the better of us:

1. We perceive an attack against our significance.

When we sense that our worth or significance is being attacked in some way, many times anger is the result. This may happen to a wife whose husband has betrayed her trust through an extramarital affair. It could be someone who feels betrayed by a friend who discusses with others something that was shared in confidence. Or it can simply be a reaction to the guy who cuts us off in traffic. We may also be overcome with anger if we feel that we are being judged unfairly or if we find ourselves in an awkward or embarrassing situation.

The bottom line is, anger results when somehow it is communicated to us that we are insignificant, unappreciated or unimportant. It is vital to understand that the greatest of human needs is the need to be loved and accepted. We were created by God with this driving force in order that He would be the One to meet this need. If we don't discover our worth and value in His love and acceptance of us, then what people do and say will always carry the potential of bringing hurt and disappointment to our lives.

2. We feel that we are losing control.

Anger also can result when we feel that we are losing power over our lives. Therefore, many times anger is an attempt to regain the feeling that we are once again in control. We often express our anger in an endeavor to control the behavior of others—whether it is the temper tantrum that leaves in its wake punched-in walls or broken household items or the more subtle "cold shoulder" silent treatment. Both responses are designed to exercise control in a situation by controlling others.

FEAR IS THE ROOT

Fear is the more powerful emotion that underlines anger and its expressions. Fear is the root of anger. Fear is the motivator for both of the responses just mentioned. Fear fuels and empowers anger. Anger must have something to which to attach itself, and it attaches itself to fear. For example, what lies behind our anger when we feel that our significance is being attacked is the *fear* of some form of rejection. The underlining force of our anger when we feel that we are losing control is the *fear* of some sort of failure.

As we settle the issue of our identity with Christ, we discover a security in His love for us. In this place of security, fear begins to lose its hold. The less fearful we are, the less authority anger has in our lives.

We can feel secure in God's love because it is perfect and unconditional. In 1 John 4:18 we read:

> There is no fear in love; but perfect love casts out fear, because fear involves torment. But he who fears has not been made perfect in love.

God's love for you transcends anything that anyone can do to you. The greater the sense of His love in our hearts, the less we feel the need to protect and control. Go to Him today. Go to the One who loves you perfectly. Let Him show you the source of your fears and the seat of your anger. Allow His love to bathe your soul, drowning out the insecurities and washing away selfish anger. As His love washes over your life, your soul will be released to soar in hope and love once again.

Chapter 6

THE FEAR OF MAN

M*ark heard a* familiar voice on the other end of the line when he answered the phone late one evening. "Mark, can we talk? I'm really concerned that our church is becoming...well, it's almost...a cult."

Mark hadn't heard from his friend Steve in three years. They had both attended the same charismatic church until Mark's career required him to relocate to another state. Consequently they had lost touch with each other. Now, in desperation, Steve was reaching out to someone outside his closely knit world.

It was clear to Mark that Steve's apprehension came as the result of his own personal observations. It was not just based on church gossip. Up to this point Steve had been careful not to discuss his thoughts with anyone. He was actually afraid to talk about the subject. Steve was particularly bothered by an attitude of secrecy concerning the church's finances.

"If anyone dares to ask a question about how the money is used, the pastor accuses him of being distrustful or disobedient," Steve explained. "And for the last three years," he added, "the pastor's sermons have almost always focused on the topic of submission to spiritual authority. If anyone leaves the church," Steve told Mark, "the pastor labels him rebellious, or he tells us he was offended."

Mark grew more concerned as Steve shared more details nervously. "The pastor also told us that since God brought us to the church, he is our spiritual father, and we should never leave unless God tells him first," Steve said. "He even told us that if we ever left without pastoral permission, we would be vulnerable to Satan's destruction."

When their conversation ended, Mark realized that his friend was trapped in an extremely unhealthy spiritual situation. He urged his friend to set up an appointment with the pastor in order to confront him about his concerns. "You can't subject yourself or your family to that kind of control, Steve," Mark advised.

A week later, when Mark talked with Steve again, Mark discovered just how strong the pastor's influence was over this congregation. Steve had confronted the pastor with his concerns. But by the end of their session together, Steve had apologized to the pastor for talking with an outsider about his problems with the church. He pledged that he would never talk with Mark again.

Mark has not heard from Steve since.

The Fear of Man

The scenario I just described is a true story—and it is much more typical than any of us would like to admit. It's a scenario that clearly demonstrates the fear of man. Though this story is one found within a church situation, the truth of the matter is that the fear of man affects every area of our lives.

In Proverbs we read, "The fear of man brings a snare, but whoever trusts in the LORD shall be safe" (Prov. 29:25). *The fear of man is really the fear of rejection.* The strongest desire we have is to be loved and accepted. We were created with this desire by God for the purpose of finding that acceptance in our relationship with Him. If we don't find acceptance in God, then we will look for that acceptance in others.

Don't misunderstand me; I know that everyone wants to be accepted and approved by others. Most people don't want to be hated or rejected by masses of people. What I am referring to is an unhealthy need for the approval of others. It is the desire to search for our identity and significance in the acceptance of man. The need for that acceptance is so powerful that we are willing to go against our conscience and better judgment to receive it. We saw that illustrated in the story about Steve and Mark. Steve was so determined to gain the approval of his pastor that he ignored the unhealthy signs of control.

The fear of man is described as a snare because we actually become captured and imprisoned by others in our need for their acceptance. We say and do things that we otherwise wouldn't do in order to gain the validation we feel we need. An extreme example of this is the initiation rites of some gangs. Many gangs require a prospective member to endure bloody beatings from the members before that person is accepted into the "fold." It is amazing that young men and women will endure these brutal attacks just for the acceptance of those in the gang and to gain a sense of identity as one of its members.

We as Christians may shake our heads in disgust at these gang rites, but we subject ourselves to the same type of cruelty. With us, though, it is manifested in relationships that strip us of our dignity and individuality. Though not physical, this abuse occurs on a much deeper level than one gang member physically attacking another. The fear of man can grip us in continuing abusive or controlling relationships where we allow others to run our lives. We may even find ourselves willing to abandon our life's purpose and to sacrifice our marriages and families—all in an attempt be accepted.

TOXIC LOVE

Insecurity and a lack of our identity in Jesus result in the fear of man. This deep-seated insecurity will produce two types of people: those who are so hungry for acceptance that they will allow others to control them, and those whose insecurities drive them to control others. Both of these types of individuals will attract each other with a magnetic pull, resulting in a codependent relationship that can eventually become destructive. I call this "toxic love." Such relationships become easily expendable. Friendships are determined by the ones we feel validate us the most, not necessarily based on truth. These individuals constantly look for validation from someone else—often someone in authority.

The Fear of Man

One example may be a person with a desperate need to be needed who is always ready to come to someone's rescue. Outwardly, this appears to be a wonderful act of benevolence. Actually, it is selfishly motivated. That person, because of a lack of identity in Jesus and the consequent insecurity, needs to be in control. If others don't respond to an act of kindness in the way that person feels they should—usually by allowing the control to continue—then the rescuer may feel hurt and rejected.

Others, out of insecurity and the need to be accepted, find themselves drawn to the controller. They are willing to abandon their individuality and to allow the controller to "run their lives." In essence, the controller becomes God to them.

There was a time in my life when I struggled with the fear of man. I had been the senior pastor of a church in Florida, a church that Bonnie and I had started in 1986. While there, I experienced a moral failure. That sounds too nice—actually, I had become addicted to pornography and consequently committed adultery numerous times by calling different escort services. I carried on with this activity for about two years. After nearly committing suicide over the shame and guilt, I confessed my double life to Bonnie. I then called a friend who was a pastor and confessed my sin to him. Shortly afterward, I resigned from my church and moved to the city where my friend was pastoring.

We became involved in the church, and I went through an extensive time of personal restoration. After two years, I became a staff member of the church. After being on staff for three years, Bonnie and I truly felt it was time to take the next step and launch out into our own ministry again. It had been a total of five years since I stepped down from the church in Florida.

The pastor was more than disappointed. He explained to us that if it was God's will for us to leave, then God would tell him, and he in turn would tell us. Until that happened, the pastor made it clear that it was our moral obligation to stay where we were. If we decided to leave, it would be against his desires, and we would be in rebellion to God, which would result in sure failure.

As in the case for most large congregations, this church was going through a season where a higher percentage of people were leaving to attend other churches.

Others in the congregation sensed the pastor's insecurity and frustration over the situation with myself and decided to take advantage by strengthening their position with him. They began to tell him that I was responsible for some of the people leaving the church because I had spoken negatively about him and had undermined his authority.

In an attempt to resolve the matter, I suggested that the pastor, those making the accusations and myself come together in a room and sort it out. I was sure that those making the accusations would not have the courage to continue their lies in front of me. But the pastor was not interested in such a meeting.

In the weeks following, I had several conversations with the pastor over this issue, but to no avail. He equated my leaving the church with my no longer loving or respecting him.

Bonnie and I started Foundation Ministries and began traveling. We were determined to continue to attend the church when we were not on the road. But the lies continued, putting ever-increasing pressure on our relationship with the church and pastor. After eight months, it seemed better for everyone involved that we move out of state, which we did.

During the time that we stayed and after we moved, out of his own pain, the pastor shared with other ministers about my "lack of character." He expressed how hurt he was that, after all he had done for me, I repaid him by sowing strife in his church. In fairness to him, I am sure he was convinced that all he had heard about me was true and that I had turned on him. I am sure that it was a very painful time for him.

Yet, I had never felt so vulnerable. Here I was, beginning a traveling ministry. My past history, to say the least, was questionable—I had been an adulterer and a liar. The man who oversaw my restoration was now saying that I had been a source of strife and contention in his church. I was afraid—and angry. I was afraid that this man's influence would be enough to shut any door of opportunity for me to preach. I knew that I couldn't defend myself. Defending yourself just makes you sound guilty, anyway. I had no past history of good character through which those hearing the lies could filter them. I felt trapped and out of control.

This was the most fearful situation I had faced in my life up to this point. I had always prided myself in being able to resolve any kind of conflict with others. Yet this was completely out of my control. Nothing I could say or do would made a difference. This situation, and my initial response to it, exposed my fear of man. It exposed my self-centeredness and my lack of trust in God. I became ensnared with anger and a sense of hopelessness. In the past, I had looked up to this man and desired his approval and acceptance. It had now become painfully clear to me that I was placing more value in his opinion of me than in God's opinion of me. I discovered that I had set someone up as a "king" in my life.

There was an instance in the Scriptures where a group of people wanted a king. Israel's desire for a king is a perfect example of humanity's need to worship and be dependent on someone other than God. When Israel requested a king God gave it. Repeatedly, God commanded Samuel to explain the process of having a king to the Israelites. As you will see in the following verses, there were trade-offs to having a king.

> And he said, This will be the manner of the king that shall reign over you: He will take your sons, and appoint them for himself, for his chariots, and to be his horsemen; and some shall run before his chariots. And he will appoint him captains over thousands, and captains over fifties; and will set them to ear [plow] his ground, and to reap his harvest, and to make his instruments of war, and instruments of his chariots. And he will take your daughters to be confectionaries, and to be cooks, and to be bakers. And he will take your fields, and your vineyards, and your oliveyards, even the best of them, and give them to his servants. And he will take the tenth of your seed, and of your vineyards, and give to his officers, and to his servants. And he will take your menservants, and

your maidservants, and your goodliest young men, and your asses, and put them to his work. He will take the tenth of your sheep: and ye shall be his servants.

—1 Samuel 8:11–17, kjv

Through Samuel, God was saying that if Israel continued in her pursuit for a king, it would result in the people giving up the rights and privileges they previously enjoyed with as God their King.

Notice Israel's response:

Nevertheless the people refused to obey the voice of Samuel; and they said, Nay; but we will have a king over us; that we also may be like all the nations; and that our king may judge us, and go out before us, and fight our battles.

—1 Samuel 8:19–20, kjv

The Israelites were willing to give up their privileges as God's people to have a king to fight their battles for them. They felt it was easier for someone else to hear from God for them than it was to take responsibility for their own relationship with God. The same is true today. Out of fear, many in life would rather have someone else as their master than to take personal responsibility for their own lives and relationship with God. It is easier to have someone else fight your battles for you. And believe me, there are plenty out there who are more than willing to take that place in your life.

If you are driven by the fear of man, then you will be subject to giving man an inordinate place in your life. A place that only belongs to Jesus. Jesus condemned such man-pleasing when he told the Pharisees: "I have come in My Father's name, and you do not receive Me... How can you believe, who receive honor from one another, and do not seek the honor that comes from the only God?" (John 5:43–44).

When we pursue the honor of men, we do so at the expense of our relationship with God. Gradually, men can take the place of God in our lives. When that happens, an unhealthy soul tie is created, and our sense of confidence is now determined by our relationships with those from whom we seek validation. Allowing another person to have this kind of control over you will destroy you spiritually, and you will always be subject to a controlling spirit.

What Israel created was a religious system that catered to man's insecurities, fueled the fear of man and empowered the controller. There is no greater example of this type of codependent relationship in Christianity than what can take place in the local church. It is within the context of the church that we are best able to observe how we relate to one another. Each local church is a separate community. Therefore, as Christians there is no better place to observe the dynamics of the fear of man and the spirit of control than within the Christian community expressed within the framework of the local church.

Many churches today struggle with varying degrees of unhealthy control—which can lead to devastating spiritual abuse if not corrected. That abuse has resulted in untold thousands of wounded and disillusioned Christians who believe they've been burned by the one institution in the world that was supposed to help them.

Don't get me wrong. I believe in the local church. The local congregation is sacred, and it is God's idea. All believers should be in fellowship with a local church according to Hebrews 10:24–25. There is a dynamic of God's grace that is only found in a consistent relationship with a healthy local body.

God's intention all along has been for the local church to be healthy, life-giving and Christ-centered. But because He has chosen to use frail, sin-prone individuals to lead His church, there is always the possibility that a local congregation can fall into deception or unhealthy spiritual patterns.

So how do the fear of man and the influence of a controlling spirit manifest in the local church?

DEADLY TRAITS OF A CONTROLLING SPIRIT

Power positioning

There is certainly a place for biblical teaching on spiritual authority. But if a pastor preaches on this subject every Sunday, constantly reminding everyone that he is in charge, you can be sure that trouble is around the corner.

If we are subject to the fear of man, the pastor actually begins to take the place of Jesus in our lives. In Steve's case, he was told that he couldn't leave his church with God's blessing unless the pastor approved the decision. The implication was that unless he received pastoral permission, God would not bless him. Controlling spiritual leaders use this kind of reasoning to manipulate people.

Some pastors may feel that the only way to measure their success is through church attendance. If they believe this, it may greatly disappoint them when people leave their church. Out of insecurity, some may actually develop a doctrine to stop people from leaving. They may preach sermons about unconditional loyalty, using the biblical stories of David and Jonathan or Elisha and Elijah. By using such examples, the leader can actually gain "biblical" grounds to control even the personal areas of the lives of his parishioners. Or a controlling leader may attempt to instill a sense of obligation by reminding his congregation of everything he has done for them. But it is the fear of man that actually gives this leader that type of control.

A true shepherd will use his influence to draw church members into a closer relationship with *Jesus*, who is the *only* "head of the church" (Eph. 5:23). A true shepherd realizes that the people in his congregation don't belong to him—they are God's flock.

Ultimately, it is my own responsibility to choose whether or not I am going to find my identity in Jesus or seek for it in someone else.

An atmosphere of secrecy

In a setting where church members have surrendered to a system of control, the leader gives limited information to each individual, carefully monitoring each relationship. As a result, each member is only able to relate to other members based on the information he has received from the leader. There is no open communication among the entire body.

Thus, if the pastor or church staff determine that one member has become a "threat," they can develop a strategy to sever that relationship—and keep the process cloaked behind a veil of secrecy. Only the information they choose to release about the incident will reach the congregation.

In unhealthy congregations, secrecy may also cloak the area of finances. Pastors may make brazen appeals for money, yet offer no assurance that the finances of the church are being handled with accountability and integrity. I even know of pastors who have told their congregations that the financial decisions of the church are not a public matter because "the congregation doesn't have the spiritual insight or maturity to understand the dynamics of church finances."

Some pastors actually preach: "It shouldn't matter to you what we do with your money—your responsibility is simply to *give.*" However, the Bible commands us to be good stewards—and part of good stewardship is making sure that proper systems of accountability are established to handle tithes and offerings.

As stewards we are responsible for where we sow our financial seed, just as a farmer is responsible for the soil in which he plants his seeds. He may have the greatest seeds possible, but if he plants them in unhealthy soil, his crop will be adversely affected. I am always surprised by those who know of unethical financial practices in their church and yet continue to give. It is clear to me that such people desire the approval of those in leadership more than they desire financial integrity.

Fear motivation

Opportunities to minister are abundant in most churches. Yet in a controlling church, ministry positions are not opportunities to serve—they are proof of one's commitment to the organization. Whether it's faithful attendance to worship services or working in some department, *loyalty* becomes the key. The results of this kind of an atmosphere are selfish ambition and competition among the people.

Church attendance is vital to our spiritual growth. But if we attend church to win the favor of the pastor or to earn his trust, then we have missed the point. Galatians 2:16 tells us that "a man is not justified by the works of the law but by faith in Jesus Christ." We cannot earn heaven or God's love. The message of God's grace doesn't cancel the need to serve—it just exposes the "why" of our service.

Even though we are instructed to engage in certain disciplines in the Christian life, these disciplines are not a means of gaining God's acceptance. They are meant to be a celebration of His unconditional love and mercy.

The pastor who tells his congregation that those who leave his church or disobey his authority are in danger of God's wrath is attempting to use fear as a carnal means of keeping people in his church. The line usually goes like this: "If you leave our church, the blessing of God will be lifted from your life, and you will miss God's will." Another version says, "If you leave our church, you will be in rebellion, and Satan will be free to bring havoc into your life."

Rather than leading his congregation with love and servanthood, the controlling pastor is trying to lead through manipulation. Fear is the motivation—not love. This type of reasoning is not from God. It is a direct contradiction to Scripture. Jesus never motivated men out of fear.

The Fear of Man

It is because we are subject to the fear of man that we find ourselves in a position to be manipulated. First John 4:18 says, "There is no fear in love; but perfect love casts out fear."

Fear-motivated control is expressed through *judgment, rejection* and *manipulation.* These leaders love conditionally. The ultimate goal of their conditional love is to see someone's conduct change or to make someone into what the leader wants that person to be. These leaders try to change another person into what the leader wants, instead of trusting God to change that person into what He wants that person to be.

People who are pulled into such an atmosphere of control will eventually display unhealthy attitudes or destructive behavior. Manipulative leaders will respond to these attitudes with rejection and judgment of the person—instead of judging the person's behavior. The leader hopes that the individual's desire for acceptance will be strong enough to cause that person to change his or her behavior. Thus an unhealthy cycle of response is present. Inadvertently, the leader is persuading the individual to live for the acceptance of man—not for the honor of God.

EMPOWERING LOVE

There are three important characteristics of God's love that we must understand to avoid any type of unhealthy relationship. These characteristics are acceptance, understanding and commitment, and they are the direct opposite of the judgment, rejection and manipulation we just discussed above.

Even though there are times where there are consequences for actions taken, we must be able to separate

95

people from their *actions.* When people know that our commitment and acceptance of them is not based on their actions, *then they are free from the need to defend themselves.* It is at this point that our prayers become effective, because love has freed them to hear and respond to the voice of God.

Allow me to give a personal example. At one point our daughter, Janae, decided that she wanted a tongue ring. Her mother and I were not excited about this, to say the least. One evening I took Janae to dinner, and we talked about her desire to have her tongue pierced. I felt that Janae was being influenced by what society said was "cool." I felt that she was finding her identity more in the world's definition of what makes someone important (at least in this situation) than she was in Christ. But I was careful not to tell her that. I just asked her to tell me her reasons for her decision. I tried to express my desire to hear and understand her.

Janae was eighteen at the time, and so I told her that obviously she was free to make her own decision. Even though we were disappointed in her decision, we affirmed our love for her. We decided that we would make sure to avoid treating her any differently than before. We did not want to display any form of rejection or judgment concerning her choice.

Janae had her tongue pierced on a Friday. The following Sunday I was ministering in another state when I received a phone call from Janae. She called to tell me that she had taken her tongue ring out, saying that she "hated it." When I arrived home, Janae explained that she had realized that her identity was more in her tongue ring than in Jesus. Though tempted, I refused to lecture her with a bunch of "I told you so's."

I believe it was because God had given us the grace to love her unconditionally that she was free to hear the voice of God for herself. As a result, her decision was based on her own conviction—not on something she needed to do to gain our acceptance.

This is how God deals with us. His unconditional love brings permanent change in our lives.

Use the following questions to determine if you are entrapped by the fear of man:

1. Have you found yourself seeking the approval of others?

2. Have you found yourself violating what you know is right in order to gain the approval of others?

3. Has a recent rejection from a friend or leader caused you to feel depressed or angry?

4. Have you found yourself looking the other way when an injustice is done because of the fear of man?

5. Have you abandoned your dreams because someone told you could never make them happen?

6. Have you found yourself pursuing relation-ships with those who you believe can validate you instead of establishing your friendships on character?

As we dare to embrace God's love for us, we free our-selves from the fear of man. When we have set ourselves free from this paralyzing fear, we find a life of great liberty. Liberty not only to pursue God's plans for our lives, but also the liberty to love others. It is impossible to truly love if we are ensnared by the fear of man. As long as we are imprisoned by the fear of man, it is difficult to know if our acts of kindness are motivated by a need for acceptance from others or because of the self-sacrificial love of God. We will never grow beyond our fear of rejection! But as we discover our identity in Jesus and His unconditional love for us, we can experience freedom from the fear of man.

Chapter 7

THE FEAR OF FAILURE

T*he high school* gymnasium was packed with anxious fans filling the room with an electrifying sense of anticipation. Each scored point was met with a victory chant that reverberated off the cement walls with a deafening echo. This was for the state championship. Glenn was in his senior year and captain of his basketball team, as well as the highest scorer in the school's history. For Glenn, this was more than a state championship game. Seated in the crowd were at least three college scouts from some of the most prestigious schools in the country. Glenn stood to gain a full scholarship and, if he continued to improve in college, maybe a chance eventually for the NBA. Never in his life did

Glenn have more at stake on just one night.

Glenn felt differently about this game for another reason. Before tonight, when he played, it was for fun. The only things he thought about were how much he enjoyed the competition and doing his best. Tonight he wondered if his best would be good enough. It was hard for him to put out of his mind all that was riding on this one game. He felt as if he were performing instead of playing.

Glenn didn't want to disappoint his dad, his coach or the scouts who came out to evaluate his playing. As the game progressed, Glenn found it increasingly more difficult to play to his normal potential. Plays that in the past were easy to execute, seemed foreign and awkward. Glenn found himself making mistakes you would normally expect a freshman to make. On top of it all, Glenn didn't score a single point during the entire first half.

The opposing team was going for the basket in an attempt to beat the half-time buzzer. Glenn had placed himself in the perfect position to snatch the rebound if the opposing player missed, at least ending the first half with his team's possession of the ball—if not a basket. He noticed the ball spinning around the rim of the basket. Glenn jumped—but not high enough. A player from the other team grabbed the rebound, then passed to another player who shot the ball from the outside, sinking it in for another two points.

The crowd for the opposing team roared with delight. As Glenn descended back to earth, he quickly crumpled to the court floor...and stayed there. When he did get up, he was favoring his right side. As he made his way back to the lockers with the rest of the team, his limp was distinct.

When Glenn's team came out of the lockers for the second half, Glenn was dressed in his sweats and sitting on the bench. Glenn insisted that he had sprained his ankle severely. Even though there was no swelling and the trainer couldn't determine that any injury had taken place, Glenn was convinced that he couldn't play the rest of the game. A day later, after X-rays had been taken, the doctors still could not find anything wrong with Glenn's ankle.

There is an expression in sports that describes what really happened to Glenn. It is called the "loser's limp." It is an athlete's way of taking himself out of the game without facing the risk of failure. In other words, he would rather feign an injury than to take the risk of failing. This way he has an excuse. The injury becomes the reason he couldn't finish what he started. He doesn't have to take responsibility for that. It's not his fault if he gets hurt. He can say, "If it wasn't for this injury, I could have been a winner."

This kind of fear is not limited just to athletics. We find it in all areas of life. We come up with a variety of circumstances beyond our control to justify quitting or not really trying. One of the best examples of the loser's limp in the Bible is found in the Gospel of Matthew. Within this parable Jesus describes how one man dealt with his fear of failure by not trying.

> Then he who had received the one talent came and said, "Lord, I knew you to be a hard man, reaping

where you have not sown, and gathering where you
have not scattered seed. And I was afraid, and went
and hid your talent in the ground, Look, there you
have what is yours."

—MATTHEW 25:24–25

The value of a talent was approximately one thousand
dollars. Can you imagine taking one thousand dollars
and burying it in a hole in the ground? That is exactly
what this man did. He may have compared what was
given to him with what the others received, feeling
insulted that he was given the least. Instead of taking the
chance of failing, this man decided to "play it safe."

He blamed his lack of productivity on his master,
saying that he was unfair and unjust. In essence, the man
who received the one talent was saying to his master, "I
could tell that you are the kind of man for whom whatever I did, it wouldn't be enough—so I did nothing."
Why did he feel like this? In his own words, this man
said that he was afraid.

In my previous book, *Finding Freedom From the Shame
of the Past*, I noted some important insights concerning
the man with the one talent:

> The servant said he was "afraid." Fear clouded his
> perspective of life. First of all, I believe that this ser-
> vant struggled with a fear of failure. The fear of
> trying, only to experience defeat. Consequently, the
> servant would rather take his chances with the
> master than face the issues within his own soul that
> sentenced him to a life of mediocrity....
>
> Another important principle is that fear caused

102

the servant to have a distorted view of the master. Fear caused this servant to automatically assume that the master was an unjust man. This fear resulted in the servant treating with contempt the thing of value that the master had entrusted to him. He took the master's money and buried it in the ground! Fear always clouds our ability to recognize those things that are of real worth. Fear causes us to treat with contempt those things that are of real value— relationships, responsibilities, marriages, families, or careers. Fear blinds us with self-absorption. We see others as the reason for our failures or difficulties, embracing a victim's mentality toward life.[1]

There is another way that the fear of failure can manifest in one's life. It is the antithesis of not trying, which is the drive for success. This drive for success can cause us to move in a frantic pace for fear that if we slow down or stop moving, failure is waiting there to capture us. It is in this place that we become power hungry and fall prey to the trappings of the very success we are pursuing. No matter how much success we achieve, we never find a place of contentment. We are never able to relax and enjoy the fruit of our labors. Fear keeps pressing us on. Yet because that fear resides in our hearts, no amount of success is able to bring the satisfaction for which we are looking. Ironically, many times it is in the midst of this success that our fear of failure is realized.

For example, in 1945 there were three men in the early stages of their ministries. Each was in his midtwenties, and all of them were experiencing varying degrees of success. Out of the three, two had achieved notable influence. Chuck Templeton and Bron Clifford were dynamos behind the pulpit. One university president, after hearing Chuck Templeton, an evangelist for Youth for Christ, preach to thousands, called him the most talented and gifted young preacher in America. In 1946 the National Association for Evangelicals published an article listing the men that had the most effective ministries in the last five years. Chuck Templeton's ministry was a major part of the article.

Bron Clifford was also believed to be someone who would have a great impact on the church world. For example, when Bron Clifford was preaching at a chapel service at Baylor University, the president of the university was so awed by Bron's preaching that he ordered the school bells turned off so that Clifford could preach without interruption.[2]

John Hagee, in his book *Lead On*, speaks of Bron Clifford:

> At the age of twenty-five, young Clifford touched more lives, influenced more leaders and set more attendance records than any other clergyman his age in American history. National leaders vied for his attention. He was tall, handsome, intelligent and eloquent. Hollywood invited him to audition for the part of Marcellus in *The Robe*. It seemed as if he had everything.[3]

In 1945, both Templeton and Clifford had started out strong. But by 1950, Templeton had left the ministry in pursuit of a career as a radio and television commentator.

Templeton eventually decided that he no longer believed in orthodox Christianity.

Bron Clifford's story is nothing short of tragic. By 1954 he had left his wife and his two Down's syndrome children. Alcohol had become the vice that destroyed his life. He wound up selling used cars in the panhandle of Texas. Nine years after being the most sought-after preacher in America, Clifford was found dead in a sleazy motel room outside the city of Amarillo, Texas.

You may be wondering who the third evangelist was. His name is Billy Graham. While Templeton and Clifford were enjoying their success, Graham was establishing boundaries within his personal life and ministry that would insure his longevity.[4]

Just recently I found a video of a preacher who ten years ago pastored one of the most influential churches in America. The video was recorded when he was at the height of his success. As I watched the video, I remembered how much I had enjoyed his preaching. The strength of the anointing that rested on his life back then was unmistakable. Yet, his marriage has since been destroyed. He has divorced his wife and married a girl who was pregnant with his child. His church has been dissolved and the building sold. Today he is still preaching, though his engagements are mostly overseas.

ISSUES OF THE HEART

What causes a man to sabotage his own success? What compels him to make decisions that cause him to self-destruct? It all comes down to "heart" issues. In Proverbs 4:23 we read, "Keep your heart with all diligence, for out of it spring the issues of life." What are the issues of the heart that are dangerous to the life of a man or woman? I don't know all of them, but do I know that much destruction comes from the insecurities fueled by a heart full of fear.

It is these very insecurities that cause us to fall prey to three dangerous attitudes of a heart driven by the fear of failure.

Ambition

This is what the apostles James and John were dealing with when they asked for positions of prominence in Mark 10:37. Ambition arises out of a deep-seated insecurity that drives us to a desperate need for the recognition of others.

Oscar Wilde once wrote, "In this world there are only two tragedies. One is not getting what one wants, and the other is getting it."

What is so seductive about ambition is the fact that it is easily interpreted as a holy desire to build the kingdom of God or as the pursuit of God's destiny for our lives. In reality, it is an attempt to add significance to our lives at the expense of others. It is blinding ambition, which rationalizes an end-justifies-the-means approach to life. When ambition sets in, we begin to define who we are by our accomplishments. We find ourselves in pursuit not just for our destiny, but for the honor of men. Jesus confronted this attitude of ambition in John 5:43–44:

> I have come in My Father's name, and you do not receive Me; if another comes in his own name, him

106

you will receive. How you can you believe, who receive honor from one another, and do not seek the honor that comes from the only God?

Sex

Insecurity can also drive us to sexual sin. No matter how much success a man achieves, insecurity will cause him to feel that something is still missing in his life. Some men will try to fill that void through sex or illicit relationships.

The drive to succeed and conquer can lead to sexual sin. This principle is illustrated in the story of King David's adulterous failure with Bathsheba. (See 2 Samuel 11.) King David knew that it was the time and the season when kings go to war. Consequently, the drive to conquer was present in David's heart. Yet, instead of expressing that desire on the battlefield, David stayed home and conquered another man's wife.

Money

In Mark 4:19, Jesus said that one of the ways Satan chokes out the fruit of God's Word in our lives is through the deceitfulness of riches. In the Book of James, we see additional insight concerning the deceit of riches.

> My brethren, do not hold the faith of our Lord Jesus Christ, the Lord of glory, with partiality. For if there should come into your assembly a man with gold rings, in fine apparel, and there should also come in a poor man in filthy clothes, and you pay attention to the one wearing the fine clothes and say

to him, "You sit here in a good place," and say to the poor man, "You stand there," or, "Sit here at my footstool," have you not shown partiality among yourselves, and become judges with evil thoughts?
—JAMES 2:1–4

Money brings a tangible influence with it. This influence attached to wealth is seductive—and often runs parallel in expression to the anointing. For example, people who are not spiritually discerning or mature will often respond to the influence of a wealthy person in the same way they respond to a person who has a strong anointing upon his or her life.

This is what was happening to the church in Jerusalem. They were showing partiality based on economic standing. The wealthy were being catered to while the poor were being overlooked.

How could anyone justify this attitude? We justify it when we begin to equate having *more stuff* with having *more of God.* The value we place on people is based on their financial standing. Many Christians justify their pursuit for wealth by thinking that an increase of finances represents an increase of God in their lives. The apostle Paul was referring to these kinds of people in 1 Timothy 6:9 when he said, "But those who desire to be rich fall into temptation and a snare, and into many foolish and harmful lusts which drown men in destruction and perdition."

THE DANGERS OF POWER

The common denominator for the three areas of ambition,

sex and money is *power.* All three are power issues. A lust for power will always show up in each of these three attitudes. We are all familiar with the saying, "Absolute power will corrupt absolutely." As old as this saying is, it is still true. Success has ruined more people than adversity ever will!

Every person has a different definition of what success is. Each person also has a different idea of how it feels to achieve success. In the same way, each person has specific moments along the road to success during which he or she is vulnerable to the temptations and snares of the enemy. But it is important to remember that a person is the most vulnerable to the seductive influences of power at the very moment that person believes he or she has achieved success.

It's interesting to note that David's sin with Bathsheba came at the end of several years of experiencing victory after victory. Every battle he fought, he won. Everything he placed his hand to turned to gold. David reached the point where he wasn't content to allow God to continue to reward him—he wanted to reward himself.

How did he reward himself? One way was to stay home when he should have been in battle. We read in 2 Samuel 11:1–2:

> It happened in the spring of the year, at the time when kings go out to battle,...one evening that David arose from his bed and walked on the roof of the king's house.

"One evening" David "arose from his bed"! While the others spent the days on the battlefield, David spent his

109

day in bed! David probably felt he had deserved this time off. But this is when Bathsheba caught his eye.

TWO MAJOR SEDUCTIONS OF SUCCESS

As we talk about the dangers of power, I want to discuss two major seductions of success that poison our hearts with pride.

The misconception of what success really is

In Psalm 75:6 we read, "For exaltation comes neither from the east nor from the west nor from the south." Promotion results in power. Power of itself is amoral. It is neither good nor evil. But it can be dangerous without proper boundaries. Power is especially dangerous when it is veiled in religion. Richard Foster states this point effectively:

> Power can be an extremely destructive thing in any context, but in the service of religion it is downright diabolical. Religious power can destroy in a way that no other power can....Those who are a law unto themselves and at the same time take on a mantle of piety are particularly corruptible. When we are convinced that what we are doing is identical with the kingdom of God, anyone who opposes us must be wrong. When we are convinced that we always use our power to good ends, we believe that we can never do wrong. But when this mentality possesses us, we are taking the power of God and using it to our own ends...When pride is mixed with power the result is genuinely volatile. Pride makes us think

that we are right, and power gives us the ability to "cram" our vision of rightness down everyone else's throat. The marriage between pride and power carries us to the brink of the demonic.[5]

In charismatic circles we often believe that when we are promoted it is because we *did something* to earn a new or greater anointing in our lives. This automatically begins to cause us to view people differently. If our homes or incomes are larger than someone else's, we think that it is because we have more of God's presence working in our lives. Or we think that we are more anointed than the other guy. This usually leads to an overexaggerated sense of importance. We express this attitude by ceasing to be thankful for the amenities of success. We begin to expect them as our "just desserts" for what we have accomplished. We begin to expect special treatment and considerations that are not afforded to everyone else unless, of course, their success is comparable with ours.

Unfortunately, it is human nature to worship men. In the church we have our celebrities, just as the world does. And sadly, our criteria for the "who's who" in the church is usually not much different from the world's criteria. Consequently, instead of the church creating an environment that challenges these subtle attitudes of pride, we cater to them. Richard Foster says, "Inordinate passions are like spoiled children and need to be disciplined, and not indulged."[6]

It is true that God rewards those who are faithful. But how He rewards us differs based on the call of God on our lives. The type of success we achieve will vary and will be dependent upon God's mission for our lives. As God sees our faithfulness in the small things, then He is able to entrust us with more. But my *more* will differ from someone else's. If God indeed causes us to prosper, it will be because we have surrendered to His will as servants—not because we earned it through self-effort.

The misconception that all increase is from God

When promotion comes from God, it increases in our sphere of influence. As a result, people's perceptions of us change, and our businesses or ministries grow. Don't misunderstand me; businesses and ministries should grow. There should be financial provision for what God has called us to do. But if we define success or promotion by this measuring stick only, we open our hearts up to a grievous deception. How people respond to us or our message in and of itself is not an indication of God's blessing. Therefore, the size or income of a ministry or business isn't a sure seal of the blessing of God.

Yet there are many preachers who feel this way. As a matter of fact, America is one of the few countries where you can market yourself and build a sizable ministry and really have nothing to say. The categorical idea that bigger is better is deadly, because it removes all the checks and balances that prevent selfish ambition.

It is also important to recognize that how people ultimately respond to a ministry isn't the litmus test to being anointed. True, the anointing is attractive. People will respond to the power of God. But they also will respond to the power of pride in a man's soul.

In His ministry, Jesus experienced extreme popularity. At times, the only place where He could accommodate the crowds who came to hear Him speak was spread over a hillside or lined upon the shore as He spoke from a boat. Yet, Jesus went from being loved and honored by the masses to being hated and jeered by the masses. Jesus experienced both extremes and was unaffected by either. He knew who He was regardless of man's response. Jesus knew He was loved and honored by the Father. He also knew that the crowds did not hold His destiny in their hands.

As a church, we have tried to hold to the values of character while pursuing success. Between these two is a thin line. How can we tell if we have crossed the line and succumbed to the seduction of inordinate power?

One major red flag is found in the area of relationships. Isolation always comes before a fall. As mentioned earlier, unbridled power can cause us to become a law unto ourselves. In Proverbs 18:1 we read, "A man who isolates himself seeks his own desires; he rages against all wise judgment." This is a man who has begun to "believe his own press." He actually believes that he is as anointed as everyone says he is. To guard and protect this great anointing, he surrounds himself with his own brand of advisors. Ones who are enamored with his success or with being on his payroll. As a result, he has insulated himself from anyone who may challenge his lifestyle or motives, and he has created a surreal world where he is untouchable and unaccountable. If this rogue individual is challenged concerning his lines of accountability, he conveniently points to his carefully selected counselors.

ESTABLISHING BOUNDARIES

What are the boundaries that are necessary to reduce the likelihood of sabotaging our own success through the fear of failure? Here are just a few.

Develop relationships with those who are not enamored with your success.

Stay in relationship with those who aren't afraid to confront attitudes of pride and arrogance that may come up in your life. At times it is difficult to recognize those who have genuine concern for you from those who want to take advantage of you. We take a risk anytime we open our lives up to someone else. But it's a risk we need to take in order to surround ourselves with men who truly can help us to navigate through the issues of life.

Proverbs 11:14 says, "Where there is no counsel, the people fall; but in the multitude of counselors there is safety."

Maintain a daily intimate relationship with God through the Scriptures and the Holy Spirit.

Don't allow the demands of your life or career to pull you away from spending time in God's presence. In Mark 3:14 we read, "Then He appointed twelve, that they might be with Him and that He might send them out to preach." The first call of the apostles was that "they might be *with* Him." It was a calling first to know Jesus, and then to go out to preach and to heal the sick. Our first calling is to know Jesus and to find our sense of worth in His love for us—not in what we do.

Maintain a heart of servanthood.

In Mark 10:43 Jesus said, "...but whoever desires to become great among you shall be your servant." Jesus went on to say that even He in His ministry wasn't called to be served, but rather to serve by giving His life as a ransom for many.

Richard Exley in his book *Perils of Power* shared a prayer with which I identify all too closely. Pray these words with me:

> Lord, I am deeply troubled by the arrogance and carnality I see in the ministry. Wealth is no longer a blessing, but a right. Your name is misused for personal gain. The trappings of worldly success have become the measurement of ministry. Lust and greed, poorly disguised, now traffic where holy simplicity once reigned. Duplicity and double talk have replaced personal integrity. Rationalization and self-justifying logic—"the ends justifies the means" kind of theology—have become the "gospel" of our day. I want to lift my voice; I want to cry out in protest; yet even as I do I sense an equally sinister spirit within. Self-righteousness tempts me to become judgmental and critical. My voice, raised in holy protest, sounds shrill and divisive even to my own ears. Help me, Lord, help me.[7]

May God guard our hearts from judgment as we pursue lives free from the seductions of success through the fear of failure.

Chapter 8

FEAR AND YOUR MONEY

Ever since he could remember, Tom was infatuated with money and the power that came with it. He studied the stock market in high school, learning all he could about the business of high finance. He read about the most powerful men in America and how each one achieved his own personal fortune—the great American dream.

Later when he gave his life to Christ, his initial intention as a businessman was to help finance the work of the kingdom of God. At least that's how it started out.

As a young Christian, Tom became part of a church that taught him that it was important for a Christian to walk in prosperity. However, although the idea of prospering as a Christian was no problem, the church's definition of prosperity was! Prosperity was defined in terms of what kind of car you drove, how large your home was, where you shopped for clothes and how large your income was. For that church, outward wealth was a sign of "how much of God" you had in your life. This philosophy was the main tenet of their teaching—it was their main emphasis.

Tom quickly recognized that the ones who fit the church's specific profile of prosperity were the ones who received the personal attention of the senior pastor. The ones who had carefully crafted an image of outward success received the positions of power in the church, becoming a part of the "blessed inner circle."

It wasn't long before Tom was able to justify a pursuit of wealth as synonymous with a pursuit for more of God in his life. He was desperate to receive the affirmation of his newfound family. Through reasoning of his own, Tom found it more and more important to create an image of a successful upwardly mobile businessman. He started his own business as a stockbroker. But rather than dealing with conventional stocks, he began trading options. He knew that although options were the most risky of investments, they were the quickest way to make "big bucks."

He was doing well, but he wasn't reaching his goal of being rich quick enough. That's when he decided to cut corners, resulting in violation of trading regulations. It wasn't long before the Federal Trade Commission discovered Tom's illegal activity. After a short period of time, they had enough evidence to freeze his accounts and seize all his assets. Tom was convicted of fraud and the misuse of funds resulting in the loss of nearly one-half million dollars for his investors. He served time in a federal penitentiary.

You may be wondering what this story has to do with fear regarding finances. It may appear to be just an example of greed. It is that. But more importantly, it is an example of fear. There is a common misconception that only the poor deal with the fear of not having enough. Often this is true. But the wealthy can also find themselves being driven with the fear of not having enough.

As you read through this chapter keep this axiom in mind: *The fear of not having enough will always translate into the love of money.* Why? Because we will pursue what we are afraid of losing, just as we pursue what we are afraid of never achieving. Consequently, this principle applies to both the wealthy and the poor.

In Mark 4:19 Jesus listed the things that can choke out the fruit of God's presence in our lives:

> And the cares of this world, the deceitfulness of riches, and the desires for other things entering in choke the word, and it becomes unfruitful.

This verse mentions the "deceitfulness of riches." *What is the deceitfulness of riches?* Or perhaps we should ask: "What causes riches to be deceitful?" What is the root of deception concerning earthly wealth? I believe that from the answers to these questions we can find freedom from fear regarding money.

In his letter to Timothy, the apostle Paul writes about the trappings found in earthly wealth:

Now godliness with contentment is great gain. For we brought nothing into this world, and it is certain we can carry nothing out. And having food and clothing, with these we shall be content. But those who desire to be rich fall into temptation and a snare, and into many foolish and harmful lusts which drown men in destruction and perdition. For the love of money is a root of all kinds of evil, for which some have strayed from the faith in their greediness, and pierced themselves through with many sorrows.

—1 TIMOTHY 6:6–10

At one point, while I was spending a considerable amount of time meditating on these verses, I asked myself the question, *How can a person fail the same life test that he or she has previously passed?* Here is what I mean by that question. In these verses Paul was talking about Christians who were pursuing wealth at the expense of their relationship with Jesus. These same people had earlier realized that nothing this world had to offer could truly satisfy them. They had come to the conclusion that no amount of money, possessions, status or power could satisfy their longing for life and peace. As a result, they had surrendered their lives to the lordship of Jesus Christ, receiving His free gift of eternal life. They had discovered the secret to true happiness and joy.

Now these same people are sacrificing this wonderful relationship with Christ for the power or influence that is attached to wealth. This is where the deception of money begins. The love of money really is a love of power—the power that money brings.

Fear and Your Money

The power that comes with money runs parallel with the power of the anointing. Because of this, it is often difficult to tell the difference. For example, an immature and undiscerning Christian will respond to a wealthy person in the same way he or she would respond to a person with a great anointing upon his life. Because such a person lacks the maturity to distinguish between these two distinct expressions of power, that person will have an inordinate interest in someone simply because of his wealth. Often this attraction will take place regardless of whether or not the wealthy are people of integrity.

The apostle James warned the churches about showing partiality based on riches:

> My brethren, do not hold the faith of our Lord Jesus Christ, the Lord of glory, with partiality. For if there should come into your assembly a man with gold rings, in fine apparel, and there should also come in a poor man in filthy clothes, and you pay attention to the one wearing the fine clothes and say to him, "You sit here in a good place," and say to the poor man, "You stand there," or, "Sit here at my footstool," have you not shown partiality among yourselves, and become judges with evil thoughts?
>
> —JAMES 2:1–4

Actually, this partiality toward the rich was the result of the power that wealth brings and the church's inability to understand the true purpose of the power of finances. What is so attractive concerning the power of money?

Its attraction and subsequent deception come as a result of finding our worth and identity in our "stuff" instead of in our relationship with Jesus. Christians are deceived into pursuing riches at the expense of their relationship with Jesus when they fail to understand that they are "departing from the faith" in their pursuit of wealth. They believe that their pursuit of wealth is a pursuit of more of God.

The Christian who believes that a pursuit of earthly wealth is a pursuit of God's presence and blessing is deceived. It is true that earthly wealth can be a blessing from God. But earthly wealth can also be obtained through hard work, creativity and perseverance.

Many of the wealthiest people in the world have absolutely no relationship with Jesus. If they were to die in their present state, they would spend eternity in hell. True, they embraced godly principles of diligence, prudence and hard work to obtain their wealth. But the goodness of Jesus is expressed to all—whether they have surrendered their lives to Him or not. The rain falls on the just and the unjust. The sun shines on the just and the unjust. It is a grave mistake to use the wealth of the world as the litmus test to determine if someone has God working in his or her life. If that were the case, then the richest people and companies in the world should be considered the most godly.

THE SAFEGUARD OF CONTENTMENT

We read it earlier, "Now godliness with contentment is great gain. For we brought nothing into this world, and it is certain we can carry nothing out. And having food and clothing, with these we shall be content" (1 Tim. 6:6–8). First of all, Paul is not making a case for a life of poverty.

He is not saying that we are to be satisfied with struggling financially and just barely getting by in life. The contentment that Paul is speaking of is a peace that comes from knowing our worth and significance are not determined by our possessions, but rather by God's love for us.

In Paul's mind, contentment was the way by which we guard our hearts from greed. Contentment is our defense from the deceitfulness of riches, which says our worth is wrapped up in our stuff, causing us to pursue wealth and sacrifice our intimacy with the Lord.

The "gain" to which Paul was referring is not measured by the standard of earthly wealth. It is a life of godliness and character accompanied by wisdom that knows what the ultimate purpose of money is to further the kingdom of God.

THE INFLUENCE OF A STEWARD

Many times Jesus taught concerning the proper place of finances in the kingdom of God. One of His many messages is found in Luke 16:1–13. Jesus begins this parable by saying:

> There was a certain rich man who had a steward, and an accusation was brought to him that this man was wasting his goods. So he called and said to him, "What is this I hear about you? Give an account of your stewardship, for you can no longer be steward."
>
> Then the steward said within himself, "What shall I do? For my master is taking the stewardship away from me. I cannot dig; I am ashamed to beg. I have resolved what to do, that when I am put out of

the stewardship, they may receive me into their houses."

So he called every one of his master's debtors to him, and said to the first, "How much do you owe my master?" And he said, "A hundred measures of oil." So he said to him, "Take your bill, and sit down quickly and write fifty." Then he said to another, "And how much do you owe?" So he said, "A hundred measures of wheat." And he said to him, "Take your bill, and write eighty." So the master commended the unjust steward because he had dealt shrewdly. For the sons of this world are more shrewd in their generation than the sons of light.

And I say to you, make friends for yourselves by unrighteous mammon, that when you fail, they may receive you into an everlasting home.

—LUKE 16:1–9

In this parable I have always found interesting the master's response regarding the steward's final actions. Scripture says that the master commended the unjust steward because of his shrewdness. The steward was clever in the way he was able to settle the master's accounts quickly. But although the steward was closing out the accounts, the master was not receiving full payment. However, if you think about it, half payment is better than nothing!

Being able to settle the master's accounts is not the reason that the unjust steward was commended. The steward's shrewdness had to do with his ability to recognize the short time in which he had influence over the master's debtors and his willingness to wield that influence to its maximum potential.

The steward knew he only had a short period of time before he would no longer have power over his master's accounts. As a steward, even though the money was not his, he had the same authority as the master over the estate. Once his stewardship was over, he would no longer possess the influence he once had. With his job coming to an end, the steward understood that his power was quickly coming to an end also. Consequently, the steward took advantage of the time he had, using his power to secure his future. By reducing the amount the debtors owed, the steward was making some friends. Friends who, I am sure, were thankful to have their debts cut in half. The steward was hoping that at a later date his newfound friends, if needed, would feel obligated to return the favor in case the steward found himself on the streets.

WE ARE STEWARDS

In Luke 16:8, Jesus says, "For the sons of this world are more shrewd in their generation than the sons of light." What does Jesus want us to learn from the unjust steward? He continues by saying, "And I say to you, make friends for yourselves by unrighteous mammon, that when you fail, they may receive you into an everlasting home" (Luke 16:9).

The phrase "when you fail" refers to when our lives are over and our time of stewardship has ended. We too are stewards. We are stewards of the mysteries of God (1 Cor. 4:1). We are also stewards of the earthly wealth we possess. As believers, all we have belongs to God.

Though we may possess money, we don't own it—He is the Master of all. We don't even own our lives.

In 1 Corinthians 4:2 we read, "Moreover it is required in stewards that one be found faithful." What Jesus wants us to see is the importance of recognizing the power that is attached to the money we have—as well as the fact that we are stewards of that power. Like the unjust steward, we only have a certain amount of time to wield that power—the span of our lifetime. Unlike the unjust steward, we are to wield that power for the sake of the kingdom—not for our own selfish gain.

Notice what Jesus says in Luke 16:10–11:

> He who is faithful in what is least is faithful also in much; and he who is unjust in what is least is unjust also in much. Therefore if you have not been faithful in the unrighteous mammon, who will commit to your trust the true riches?

What is "the least" to which Jesus is referring? Money. In other words, if we cannot guard our hearts from the deception of the power attached to money—a power that is temporary—we will never be able, with integrity, to wield the power of the anointing, which is a greater power and carries eternal value. How do we demonstrate our faithfulness concerning "that which is least"? By giving.

Giving is a tangible expression of our trust in God as our provider. Giving is a tangible expression of our understanding concerning the purpose of finances. If our hearts have been captured by fear, then we will see giving as *subtraction*. Each time we write a check to the

126

work of the gospel, fear will cause us to view that money as leaving our lives.

I am convinced that it is not rebellion that causes most people not to give consistently—it is fear. In Genesis 15:1, God spoke to Abraham, "Do not be afraid, Abram. I am your shield, your exceedingly great reward." Up to this point, Abraham had viewed his possessions as his shield. God removed Abraham's fear by showing him that He could protect him better than his wealth ever could. Many Christians, like Abraham, view the money they possess as a shield against poverty and lack.

If the fear of never having enough money translates into the love of money, that fear will cause us to hold on desperately to what we have. That's why greed, through fear, can grip the heart of the poor just as easily as the heart of the rich.

People who find security or identity in what they have can, at times, appear to be very giving and generous people. But remember, it is fear that causes them to define themselves by what they own. In the same way, fear drives them to pursue wealth as an indicator of their spirituality. Yet, it is impossible to give and, at the same time, to pursue riches. Jesus said:

> No servant can serve two masters; for either he will hate the one and love the other, or else he will be loyal to the one and despise the other. You cannot serve God and mammon [money].
> —Luke 16:13

Though such a person may appear to be generous, that person is not really *giving*—he is *buying*. These people buy friendships, favors and positions under the guise of benevolence. What is the difference? It is the motive of the heart.

Many times a selfish heart motive can be exposed by observing to whom we are giving. This is what Jesus did with the rich young ruler. Jesus asked him to give all that he had to the poor. In other words, to give to those who could never do anything for him in return. The young ruler's response? "But he was sad at this word, and went away sorrowful, for he had great possessions" (Mark 10:22). In reality, he didn't have the great possessions— the great possessions had him!

RELEASING THE POWER OF FINANCES

When it comes to God's kingdom, the money we give becomes our shield against poverty and lack, not the money we keep. Not the money itself, but through our giving, we express our faith in God as our provider, the One who shields us from lack.

As we give we release the power attached to finances for the sake of the kingdom. We need to respect the influence attached to our finances enough to wield that influence through consistent giving. This is the kind of giving that Jesus respects and honors. In Mark 12:41–44 we see this kind of giving demonstrated:

> Now Jesus sat opposite the treasury and saw how the people put money into the treasury. And many who were rich put in much. Then one poor widow came and threw in two mites, which make a quadrans. So He called His disciples to Himself and said

to them, "Assuredly, I say to you that this poor widow has put in more than all those who have given to the treasury; for they all put in out of their abundance, but she out of her poverty put in all she had, her whole livelihood."

The widow woman didn't have much to give—just two mites. A mite was a small copper coin, each one worth just a fraction of a penny. But even with what little she had, she recognized its value. She could have rationalized away not taking advantage of her opportunity to give by convincing herself that she couldn't do without what little she did have. Instead, she wielded the influence of what she possessed to the maximum for the sake of others. She wasn't afraid to trust God with her future. It was her offering that Jesus honored. It wasn't the amount that caught the heart of Jesus. It was the heart behind her giving.

The others gave out of their abundance. They gave what they would never miss. The offerings that were given by the wealthy didn't require faith in God as their provider. There was no sacrifice involved. They gave what was convenient; she gave what was necessary.

Please don't misunderstand me; I am not making a case for people to give to the point of being irresponsible concerning their financial obligations. But I am talking about giving to the point where it is a genuine expression of faith.

Perhaps the best example that I have recently heard of true biblical giving occurred in Africa. A man with whom I am acquainted is the head of a missions organization dedicated to the training of pastors on the continent of Africa. Several times a year, his missions ministry holds conferences to provide materials and training that ordinarily would not be available to African pastors.

One week they held a special meeting in Malawi, one of the poorest countries in the world. The pastors there have almost no money. Nevertheless, one pastor believed that God had instructed him to give an offering to the missions ministry.

For an entire year his church received offerings and collected clothing to give to the head of the organization. After a year the offerings totaled what would amount to about fifty dollars in U.S. currency. On the day of the meeting, this pastor presented the leader with the offering—and the clothes his church had faithfully collected. But he didn't stop with that. He then proceeded to tell the leader that during the previous night, God had visited him and challenged him to take his giving one step further.

At that point, the pastor took off his most valuable possession—his watch—and placed it on the table with the offering. This simple act caused a beautiful spirit of love and generosity to be released, and the other pastors began to place different items of personal value on the table. Some had only the clothes they were wearing and their Bibles, so they took off their shirts and ties. Some even gave their Bibles as an offering.

I have had the occasion to relate this story a few times. On two occasions, an individual who heard the story gave me an offering for the pastor from Malawi. Neither offering was large by American standards. But just one of those offerings was the equivalent of a year's salary for the pastor from Malawi.

This is the point: Like the widow woman, when this pastor gave his offering, he wasn't giving to get. He had no idea that someone in America, whom he would never meet, would hear his story of obedience. He gave because of his love for God and the leader of the missions organization.

This is the essence of true giving. When we become overwhelmed with His love for us, we are convinced that He is a perfect provider. Fear of not having enough fades in the light of God's love. His love seals our hearts with His peace and contentment, freeing us from the drive to pursue riches. Instead, we pursue faithfulness.

Chapter 9

A HEART OF FEAR
OR A HEART OF FAITH?

I*n chapter four* we discovered that when the Scriptures refer to the heart, they are referring to the functions of the spirit and soul of a person. The heart is a combination of the spirit and soul. Our spirits are re-created after the perfect image and likeness of God—a fact that is imperative for us to know. Our souls need to be renewed and transformed into the image of Jesus. It is because we are able to draw from the perfect nature of Jesus that we can experience the transformation of our souls (mind, will and emotions), thus enabling us to find freedom from the prison of any damaging emotion—the most powerful of which is fear.

If the heart referred only to an individual's born-again

spirit, there wouldn't be a need to guard and protect it since the born-again spirit is re-created in God's perfection. For example, in Proverbs 4:23 we are commanded to "keep your heart with all diligence, for out of it spring the issues of life."

In the same way, if the heart referred to the spirit of a man only, then it wouldn't have the capacity to be hardened. Yet in Proverbs 28:14 we read, "Happy is the man who is always reverent, but he who hardens his heart will fall into calamity." Mark 6:52 speaks of the disciples after the miracle of the loaves by saying, "For they had not understood about the loaves, because their heart was hardened."

Because the heart refers to both the spirit and the soul of a person, the heart therefore becomes the pivotal issue of our lives. This is why the Scriptures say that out of the heart "spring all the issues of life" (Prov. 4:23).

THE HEART

The Scriptures that most exhaustively describe the function of the heart are found in the fourth chapter of Mark, within the teaching of the parable of the sower. Verses 1–12 contain Jesus' teaching about the power of the heart. In verses 13–20 He explains the parable to His disciples. Within Jesus' explanation of this teaching, we discover how crucial a part the heart plays in our relationship with God and His Word.

In the parable of the sower Jesus describes a man who sows seed into four different types of soil. The seed represents the Word of God. The soil represents the heart. Four different types of heart responses are described by

A Heart of Fear or a Heart of Faith?

Jesus using the illustration of four different types of soil.

The unperceiving heart

In Mark 4:3–4 we read about the first type of heart upon which the seed of the Word fell:

> Listen! Behold, a sower went out to sow. And it happened, as he sowed, that some seed fell by the wayside; and the birds of the air came and devoured it.

This is the heart that hears the Word of God but has no capacity to receive the truths of the Word. People with this kind of heart see, but they do not perceive. They hear, but they do not understand. Jesus described them as the kind of spiritual soil that, after the seed is sown, Satan is immediately able to come and steal the Word of God from their heart.

The heart without roots

Then Jesus described a second type of heart.

> These likewise are the ones sown on stony ground who, when they hear the word, immediately receive it with gladness; and they have no root in themselves, and so endure only for a time. Afterward, when tribulation or persecution arises for the word's sake, immediately they stumble.
> —MARK 4:16–17

These are the people who quickly get excited about the truths they have initially discovered in the Scriptures. But when they begin to experience hardship or persecution because of the Word of God, they just as quickly become

135

offended over the very truths about which they were previously excited. Jesus described them as shallow. The soil of their heart was hard, so consequently the Word was able to be active only on a surface level in their lives. As a result, it didn't take much for the winds of adversity to uproot what fruit they did have.

The neglectful heart

Jesus described a third type of heart condition:

> Now these are the ones sown among thorns; they are the ones who hear the word, and the cares of this world, the deceitfulness of riches, and the desires for other things entering in choke the word, and it becomes unfruitful.
>
> —MARK 4:18–19

These individuals are the ones who at one time were producing fruit in their lives. But somewhere along the way, they had become neglectful in tending to the garden of their hearts. In a natural garden, if it is not tended to, weeds and thorns will grow up and choke out the fruit of the garden. In the same way, these neglectful hearts have allowed the weeds and thorns of worry, lust for money and the things of the world to come in and choke out the fruit in the garden of their hearts.

The harvesting heart

Finally, Jesus described a fourth type of heart in Mark 4:20, which says:

> But these are the ones sown on good ground, those

who hear the word, accept it, and bear fruit: some
thirtyfold, some sixty, and some a hundred.

With this verse, Jesus is declaring the possibility for all
of us here on this earth to produce a hundredfold harvest
of God in our lives. He is not indicating some God-
ordained degrees of potential harvest for believers. It is a
fallacy to think that there are some who are destined to
produce only a thirtyfold harvest, others sixty and a few
rare ones who are destined to produce a hundredfold. By
mentioning degrees of thirty, sixty and a hundredfold,
Jesus was saying that the response of your heart to His
Word will determine your harvest. Some will respond
with only a thirtyfold desire for a harvest. Others will
make a hundredfold response—and reap a hundredfold
harvest. The heart determines the harvest.

The emphasis of this parable is not about the *seed of
God's Word*, but rather about the *soil of the heart*. There is
a phrase that Jesus used as He taught on the subject of
the heart. The first time we see this phrase is in Mark 4:9
where Jesus says, "He who has ears to hear, let him
hear!" This phrase is repeated in verse 23: "If anyone has
ears to hear, let him hear." Again in verse 24 Jesus says,
"Take heed what you hear."

Jesus knew that the way we choose to hear the Word is
the determining factor to how the Word will work in our
lives. Here is a vital key: *When it comes to the Word of God,
we don't hear with our ears—we hear with our heart.*

For example, in Isaiah 55:10–11 God speaks through
the prophet, explaining how His Word works. God
illustrates this process by describing the rain and snow

falling from heaven to the earth:

> For as the rain comes down, and the snow from heaven, and do not return there, but water the earth, and make it bring forth and bud, that it may give seed to the sower and bread to the eater, so shall my word be that goes forth from My mouth; it shall not return to Me void, but it shall accomplish what I please, and it shall prosper in the thing for which I sent it.
>
> —Isaiah 55:10–11

A pastor friend of mine described to me how as he meditated on these verses it occurred to him that rain and snow don't technically *fall* from the heaven. They are actually *pulled* from the heavens by the force of gravity. The same force of gravity holds the rain and snow in the earth so that the soil with its seeds can receive the necessary nutrients. As a result, the fertile soil of the earth begins to bear fruit. The nutrients saturate the earth, causing it to bring forth life and bud, producing "seed for the sower and bread for the eater" (NIV).

In verse 11 God is affirming that this is the way His Word works in our heart: "So shall My word be that goes forth from my mouth." God has spoken. He has spoken to us through His Word. Just as gravity places a demand on the rain and snow, pulling them to the earth, in the same way, to truly "hear" we must place a demand on the Holy Spirit to teach us the truths of His Word. But how we hear with our heart will determine our harvest. A hungry heart and a teachable spirit are the "gravity" that places the necessary demand on the Spirit to teach us.

A Heart of Fear or a Heart of Faith?

For this reason, two people can attend the same church, hear the same sermons and read the same Bible; yet one matures year after year while the other struggles with the same issues year after year. If the church, the teaching and the Bibles are the same, what is the difference? It is the condition of their hearts. One used the gravity of a hungry heart to place a demand—or a pull, if you will—on the Word. The other did not. In other words, just showing up at church to hear a sermon or reading your Bible does not exert enough "spiritual gravity" to mature you in the Word!

HOW ARE YOU SOWING?

Jesus continued His teaching about the heart by saying:

> Take heed what you hear. With the same measure you use, it will be measured to you; and to you who hear, more will be given. For whoever has, to him more will be given; but whoever does not have, even what he has will be taken away from him.
>
> —MARK 4:24–25

The phrase "more will be given" in verse 24 is the translation of the Greek word *prostithemi*. The prefixed preposition *pros* means "toward." The idea being conveyed is that more will be added to that which is your due. This implies that the reward will be out of proportion to the virtue and knowledge acquired. The translation from *Word Studies in the Greek New Testament* says:

> Keep an ever watchful eye on what you are hearing. In the measure by which you are measuring, it will

be measured to you; and it will be measured to you not only according to that measure, but there will be some added on top of that. For he who has, it shall be given to him. And he who does not have, even what he has shall be taken away from him.[1]

Again, in these verses we see that the way we sow the seed of God's Word in our hearts is important. As we measure out, or set into motion, God's Word in our hearts, we actually receive more of His life and wisdom back in return. But notice again what verse 25 says: "For whoever has, to him more will be given; but whoever does not have, even what he has will be taken away from him."

What does it mean: "for whoever has...more will be given"? It means that the one who recognizes and values what he has in the form of the seed of the Word—and consistently sows that seed—will receive more. This verse goes on to say, "Whoever does not have, even what he has will be taken away from him." Perhaps you are thinking, *How can someone lose what he does not have?* This verse is referring to those who, because of their heart condition, don't have the wisdom to recognize the value of the Word that has been given them and therefore do nothing with it. As a result, they lose the opportunity to strengthen and increase what they once possessed.

We can see this same principle in the natural. When we stop using certain muscles, they begin to atrophy over time. They become weaker, and they shrink in size and strength. In other words, in the same manner whereby we produce an abundant harvest when we are diligent in sowing the seed of God's Word in our hearts, negligence will destroy the power of the seed of God's Word in our hearts.

WHAT ARE YOU SOWING?

In this parable Jesus also communicated to us the importance of understanding what we are sowing. A while ago, as I meditated on this portion of Scripture in Mark 4, something occurred to me that I had never noticed before. Jesus used a *natural* system to describe how the Word of God works in our hearts—as opposed to a *social* system.

A social system is a system established and governed by the values and ideologies of men. For example, our judicial system is a social system. It has been established by the values of men—particularly the value that everyone is presumed innocent until proven guilty by a court of law. Another example of a social system is our government. It too has been established and governed by the values of men. Because a social system is governed by the values of men—who are flawed with natural human weaknesses—it can be cheated or manipulated.

My wife, Bonnie, subscribes to *Reader's Digest*. Every now and then, I will pick up an issue and read portions of it. I have my favorite sections, one of which is a section titled "That's Outrageous!" This section is a collection of different examples of weaknesses in the judicial system. By reading this section you may find yourself reading about a man who killed a dog and received ten years in prison while another man killed three people and was out of prison in three years. After you read these

141

stories, you find yourself saying under your breath, "That's outrageous!"

The reason these injustices exist is because our judicial system is a social system; therefore, it can be cheated or manipulated. Because it is established on the values of mere men, there is room for weaknesses and loopholes. A good attorney understands this fact, and consequently he knows how to "work the system" to the advantage of his client.

Another example of a social system is our educational system. How many of you ever crammed for an exam when you were in school—and passed it? I certainly did. But how many would pass that same exam if you were to take it one week later? Probably very few. If it is possible to cram for a test and receive a passing grade, then it stands to reason that we could go through our whole high school career, cramming for tests, getting passing grades, but not really changing. Why? Because we never really learned the material. We just "worked the system." In the end, we knew no more of the material than when we first started class.

There is a reason why Jesus didn't use a social system when describing the process of the Word of God as it works in our hearts. He used a natural system—farming. The seasons of the earth that govern farming were established by a perfect and eternal God. The laws of farming are unchanging. Therefore it is a system that can't be cheated or manipulated. A farmer cannot decide to plant his seed in September and reap a harvest in October. He cannot ignore the laws of nature that dictate the action he needs to take to raise his crops. All that farmer can do is observe the laws of nature, and then surrender himself to the authority of the system—that is, if he wants a harvest.

In the same way, the process by which the heart works is a system that can't be cheated. The irrevocable truth of the matter is that whatever we sow in our hearts, we will harvest in our lives! We can cram for tests in school, but we can't cram and expect to pass the tests of life. The problem is, we want to approach our Christianity in the same way we approached school. Many people want to harvest differently than what they have sown, assuming they can harvest where they haven't sown. It just doesn't work that way.

What does this have to do with fear? Allow me to explain.

Starting in January of 1999, there was a lot of talk and speculation concerning the potential problems of Y2K. Many of the cries of the doomsayers came from the camp of Christianity. Preachers declared that we would experience the end of all that we have previously known in our world. Some went to the extreme of encouraging their parishioners to liquidate their assets and buy gold, since paper money would be useless. These prophets were saying that because of faulty computer chips, we would be without water and electricity and would be unable to purchase food. As a result, they conveniently set up the business of selling gold, as well as selling one- to two-year supplies of freeze-dried food, generators and other survival-related goods.

I read the story in a local suburban paper of one couple who decided to cash in on the Y2K hysteria.

They opened a store selling everything anyone would find necessary to survive the catastrophe and stock their homes in an attempt to secure their futures.

Many Christians with whom I spoke about the stockpiling of food and equipment told me quickly that they were not doing it out of fear. They felt they were simply being prudent in preparing themselves for an uncertain future. Some quoted Proverbs 22:3, which says, "A prudent man foresees evil and hides himself, but the simple pass on and are punished." It seemed to make sense to many at the time. Other Christians came up with catchy bumper-sticker-type phrases like, "Don't panic, just prepare." Some spoke of this crisis as being a great opportunity to evangelize the lost by sharing their food and goods with them during the inevitable crises to come.

The problem I had with the preaching of the Y2K message was that it was a "gospel" that wasn't transcultural. In other words, there were only certain countries where this message would even apply. You would have great difficulty getting the people groups of many Third World countries concerned about a world without the modern conveniences of life. If the doomsayers attempted to preach their Y2K message to these people, they would probably respond by saying, "And your point is...? We already have to boil water, sleep on a dirt floor, live by the light of a fire and hunt for our own food. And, by the way, what is a computer?"

The truth of the matter is that here in America we feared the loss of our comfortable lifestyle. A lifestyle to which we have become accustomed, and one in which, sad to say, we find our identity. Consequently, all of this preparation smacked of a spirit of self-preservation, which is the gate through which fear first entered the heart of man in the Garden.

The couple mentioned earlier who owned their own Y2K survival store were asked by the reporter of their local paper what they would do if Y2K proved to be nothing but hype. Their response was similar to what I heard from so many other Christians: "We will give these provisions away to missionaries."

Here's the point. In a moment, you can easily give the stuff you have collected for eighteen months away to missionaries. But you cannot sow fear in your heart for eighteen months and then, in a moment, get rid of that fear. You may no longer be afraid of Y2K, but that fear will show up in some other area of your life. You can count on it. Why? Because the system of sowing and reaping concerning the heart, like the natural system of farming, can't be cheated. "Do not be deceived, God is not mocked; for whatever a man sows, that he will also reap" (Gal. 6:7). Whatever we put in our heart is the harvest we receive.

THE POWER OF THE UNSEEN

The heart is designed to produce what is sown into it. If we sow the seed of God's Word, it will result in a heart of faith in God. Like fear, faith is a spiritual and tangible force. Faith is a heart expression of trust in something or someone. The truth of the matter is that we are believing something all the time—positive or negative. Either we are expressing faith in the voice of the world, of sickness, of poverty and defeat, or we are believing in the integrity of God's promises to us of life, courage, healing and blessing. This heart expression of trust is the force of faith. Therefore, faith is a force that is either moving us toward peace and victory, or it is moving us toward fear and defeat.

As I have already stated, we can choose to live our lives by worldly faith. The faith of the world places trust in what it already can see, believing that what is seen is the final word. Biblical faith is the opposite. For example, in Hebrews 11:1 we read, "Faith is the substance of things hoped for, the evidence of things not seen." The Amplified Bible translates this verse this way:

> Now faith is the assurance (the confirmation, the title deed) of the things [we] hope for, being the proof of things [we] do not see and the conviction of their reality [faith perceiving as real fact what is not revealed to the senses].

The mistake we often make is to think that what is unseen is not real. For example, you can't see faith. But you can see the evidence of faith. In other words, by our own words and actions we reveal that in which we have placed our faith and trust. But you can't see the essence of the force of faith itself.

Faith in God perceives as real fact what is not perceived to the senses. With this thought in mind, one very important aspect of biblical faith is clear to our understanding: *When it comes to the things of the kingdom of God, what we can't see carries more weight than what we can see.* This truth is clearly stated in the teaching on the parable of the sower. Once a farmer plants his seed, that seed is initially hidden under the earth. But because the man who sows the seed understands the laws of farming, he knows that in the darkness of the unseen, under the earth, something powerful is happening.

Jesus was constantly challenging us to value the unseen over the seen.

> Take heed that you do not do your charitable deeds before men, to be seen by them. Otherwise you have no reward from your Father in heaven...But when you do a charitable deed, do not let your left hand know what your right hand is doing, that your charitable deed may be in secret; and your Father who sees in secret will Himself reward you openly.
> —MATTHEW 6:1, 3–4

The message here is clear. True faith is trusting in God to reward us. It is those things done in secret that the Father is able to reward. The things that we do in order to gain the approval and acceptance of man—no matter how charitable—cannot and will not be rewarded by our heavenly Father. By demonstrating our piety before men in order to be seen by men, we have in essence rewarded ourselves. When we sow in secret, we are trusting in God—not man. We are demonstrating our assurance that our heavenly Father is faithful to reward our faithfulness. Why? Because a law of faith is this: *When you sow in secret, what you can't see carries more weight than what you can see.*

THE POWER OF PATIENCE

Another aspect to biblical faith is the principle of time.

147

When it comes to the things of the kingdom of God, there is something more powerful than the immediate. We live in such an instant society consisting of microwaves, fast food, faxes, cell phones and computers. All of these tools are designed to enable us to govern our lives and businesses with greater speed and efficiency. The overwhelming message is, "You don't have to wait." Time has become man's number one enemy. I, along with everyone else, enjoy the conveniences of modern technology. But these conveniences have affected our mind-set concerning our relationship with God. As a result, many times we attempt to dictate an "instant" relationship with God.

When it comes to technology, we can afford to attempt to beat the clock. But to approach our relationship with God in the same way can be deadly. Being able to embrace time as our friend is crucial to living a life of faith toward God.

In Mark 4:26–28, Jesus taught a parable concerning the process of the kingdom of God.

> The kingdom of God is as if a man should scatter seed on the ground, and should sleep by night and rise by day, and the seed should sprout and grow, he himself does not know how. For the earth yields crops by itself: first the blade, then the head, after that the full grain in the head.

Notice that after the seed of the Word is sown, it is first the blade that appears, then the head, then over time the full corn in the head. The farmer knows that each passing day brings him one day closer to his harvest. This should be our attitude. Yet many Christians view the passing of each day as taking them further from the harvest of God's promises.

It is impossible to live a life of biblical faith without surrendering to the force of patience. In Luke 21:19 Jesus said, "By your patience possess your souls." In James 1:4 we read, "But let patience have its perfect work, that you may be perfect and complete, lacking nothing." If you have sown the seed of God's Word, then you can afford to view time as your friend.

Allow me to illustrate this point with some information about the Chinese bamboo tree. The seed of this tree is very unusual. Once the seed of the Chinese bamboo tree has been planted, the only thing you see for four years is a small sprout with a bud at the end. Four years! I'm not much of a plant guy, but if I did not understand the process of this seed, I would be greatly discouraged about the growth of this tree if all I saw for four years was a bud! But over that time, in the place of the unseen, an intricate root system is developing. This root system is preparing to support a superstructure, because from year four to year five the Chinese bamboo tree will grow up to eighty feet—in one year!

This is a perfect illustration of the kingdom of God. As a matter of fact, Jesus used a similar illustration in Mark 4:30–32, where He said:

> To what shall we liken the kingdom of God? Or with what parable shall we picture it? It is like a mustard seed which, when it is sown on the ground, is smaller than all the seeds on the earth; but when it is sown, it grows up and becomes greater than all

herbs, and shoots out large branches, so that the birds of the air may nest under its shade.

When you are sowing the Word of God in your heart, you may be longing to see a great explosion of spiritual growth on the outside—extending your branches out to provide spiritual shelter for those around you. But relax! Time is your friend. There is an intricate foundation, a root system to support a superstructure forming deep within. Your fifth year is coming.

Chapter 10

A CHILD OF THE LAW
OR A SON OF LOVE?

In the Book of Galatians, the apostle Paul deals with the Law—a subject that affects the life of every Christian. This subject has the potential to bring us into a place of liberty and power or to imprison us in a place of fear and bondage. The Law ignites fear and keeps it alive in the heart of man.

In this chapter, we will look closely at what the apostle Paul means when he refers to the Law. We will also see what the Law means to us as New Testament believers. As we explore the issue of the Law and how it empowers fear in man, we will observe a series of important contrasts in the Book of Galatians:

- A "different type gospel" vs. the authentic gospel

- Man's reasoning vs. God's revelation
- Law vs. grace
- Works vs. faith
- The curse of death vs. the blessings of life
- Condemnation vs. acquittal
- Defeat vs. victory
- The Old Covenant vs. the New Covenant
- Living in the flesh vs. walking in the Spirit
- Servants of bondage vs. sons of freedom

A PEOPLE SEDUCED

Galatia was a Roman province located in what now would be southern Turkey. Paul had planted churches in the province of Galatia during his first missionary journey. Paul considered his time there a great success, remarking in Acts 14:27 that the "door of faith" had been opened to the Gentiles. He also visited the regions of Galatia on his second and third journeys. Paul's letter to the Galatian Christians was in response to the teaching of a religious group known as the Judaizers, who had come to the province of Galatia and had begun to teach the Galatian Christians that to be accepted by God they needed to be circumcised. They also taught that the Galatians must observe the Law of Moses.

These traditional Jewish teachers refused to accept the teaching and the authority of the apostles concerning the acceptance of the Gentile believers. The apostles and elders in Jerusalem had settled the issue of allowing Gentiles to become a part of the kingdom without the observance of the Law or requiring circumcision. The Jerusalem leaders had communicated their decision in a

152

letter addressed to the Gentile believers in Antioch, Syria and Cilicia. In this letter they wrote:

> Since we have heard that some who went out from us have troubled you with words, unsettling your souls, saying, "You must be circumcised and keep the law"—to whom we gave no such commandment—it seemed good to us, being assembled with one accord, to send chosen men to you with our beloved Barnabas and Paul, men who have risked their lives for the name of our Lord Jesus Christ. We have therefore sent Judas and Silas, who will also report the same things by word of mouth. For it seemed good to the Holy Spirit, and to us, to lay upon you no greater burden than these necessary things: that you abstain from things offered to idols, from blood, from things strangled, and from sexual immorality. If you keep yourselves from these, you will do well.
>
> —Acts 15:24–29

In spite of this official statement from the elders and apostles in Jerusalem, the Jewish traditionalists felt they had a corner on the market concerning Jesus. They undermined the influence of Paul by saying that he was not really an apostle. They said his teachings were taken secondhand from the apostles at Jerusalem, therefore they could not be trusted. When the apostle Paul heard about the Judaizer's influence on the churches in Galatia, he responded by writing a letter. Within his epistle, he addresses the accusations made about him by the Judaizers, as well as his concerns for the Galatians' welfare.

Paul couldn't believe that the Galatians were so easily influenced by the legalistic teachings of these heretics. In Galatians 1:6 Paul says, "I marvel that you are turning away so soon from Him who called you in the grace of Christ, to a different gospel…" As far as Paul was concerned, the Galatians were giving heed to a false gospel, a perverted expression of the true gospel.

> …which is not another [gospel]; but there are some who trouble you and want to pervert the gospel of Christ. But even if we, or an angel from heaven, preach any other gospel to you than what we have preached to you, let him be accursed. As we have said before, so now I say again, if anyone preaches any other gospel to you than what you have received, let him be accursed.
>
> —GALATIANS 1:7–9

It is clear that Paul felt strongly that the teachings of the Judaizers were not from God and were designed to imprison the Gentile believers in a legalistic system that could only result in a powerless Christianity. It didn't matter to him who preached another type of gospel—even if it were an angel. They were not to receive it. It is clear that Paul felt strongly concerning the message he taught while he was in Galatia. In Galatians 1:11–12, Paul refers to the source of his teaching, saying:

> But I make known to you, brethren, that the gospel which was preached by me is not according to man. For I neither received it from man, nor was I taught it, but it came through the revelation of Jesus Christ.

154

A Child of the Law or a Son of Love?

The apostle Paul was confident that what he had preached to them was the true gospel. It was a gospel not after the traditions of men, but one that was revealed to him by Jesus Christ Himself. Paul's message had come by the revelation of the Holy Spirit.

This issue with the Judaizers regarding the source of his message was one with which Paul had to deal throughout his ministry. In his defense of his message here in the Book of Galatians, Paul explains his call to the ministry after his encounter with Jesus on the road to Damascus. Regarding the chain of events that took place after his conversion, Paul writes:

> I did not immediately confer with flesh and blood, nor did I go up to Jerusalem to those who were apostles before me; but I went to Arabia, and returned again to Damascus. Then after three years I went up to Jerusalem to see Peter, and remained with him fifteen days. But I saw none of the other apostles except James, the Lord's brother.
> —GALATIANS 1:16–19

Paul had spent three years following his conversion being tutored by Christ Himself. No man had opened up the message of the gospel and prepared Paul for his work of evangelism—Christ had prepared Him. The gospel he taught was the gospel of Christ. After the completion of the three years, Paul finally went to Jerusalem where he met with the apostle Peter, remaining with Peter fifteen days. He also met with James, the brother of Jesus. Then again, fourteen years later, Paul made his way back to Jerusalem with Titus to explain the revelation he had received concerning the grace of God.

While in Jerusalem, he met with the leaders of the church in Jerusalem, including Peter, to submit his teaching to them for correction. From Acts 15 we know that the leaders confirmed that Paul's revelation and ministry to the Gentiles were indeed of God, and they blessed Paul in his endeavors to reach the Gentiles.

Yet, while Paul was in Jerusalem, a sect of legalistic Jews challenged Paul's message. This challenge would be the beginning of a persecution that Paul would experience for the rest of his life and ministry.

Paul speaks of this meeting with the legalistic Jews in Galatians 2:3–5:

> Yet not even Titus who was with me, being a Greek, was compelled to be circumcised. And this occurred because of false brethren secretly brought in (who came in by stealth to spy out our liberty which we have in Christ Jesus, that they might bring us into bondage), to whom we did not yield submission even for an hour, that the truth of the gospel might continue with you.

These Judaizers declared to Titus, a Gentile, that if he wanted truly to be accepted by God, he needed to be circumcised. Titus felt no compulsion to do so, and Paul certainly was not going to encourage Titus in this direction. Paul was convinced that justification came by grace through faith alone, and not through the observance of the Law. This challenge by the Judaizers in Jerusalem became a precedent for the kind of confrontation Paul encountered again and again throughout his ministry. Legalistic Jews would spy out Paul's meetings, listening to his teachings. Then after Paul left, they would come in and subvert Paul's message. In this way, Paul was out of the picture—he couldn't defend his teaching. This is exactly what happened in Galatia.

I believe that this was Paul's thorn in the flesh. Many theologians believe that Paul's thorn was some type of sickness or disease. Yet Paul himself mentioned that his greatest challenge was his concern for the condition of the church. In 2 Corinthians 11:28, Paul expresses the weight of his concern for the churches, saying, "Besides the other things, what comes upon me daily: my deep concern for all the churches."

It is interesting to note that wherever Paul went, his greatest source of persecution came not from the Gnostics or the Roman government or the Greeks, but as a result of the religious teachings from the legalists.

THE LAW

The point of contention between the legalists and Paul's message was rooted in the Law. What exactly was the Law, and why did it present such a problem for the early Christians? What Law was Paul referring to when he mentioned the Law? When Paul mentions the Law, he is referring to the Mosaic Law. In order to understand how the Mosaic Law affects our relationships with God— even today—let's look closely at this Law of Moses.

The Law to which these legalists referred is found in the first five books of the Old Testament—Genesis, Exodus, Leviticus, Numbers, Deuteronomy. It involved much more than the Ten Commandments, which do not contain all of the Law. The Law, as found in these first five books, was divided into three categories: the moral law, types and shadows and the social law.

The moral law

The moral law is the body of rules and regulations known as the Ten Commandments. It is divided into two parts. The first five commandments deal with our relationship with God, and the last five commandments deal with our relationships with others. It was through these rules that the Jews were to govern themselves.

Obviously, it is impossible to keep perfectly the Ten Commandments, thereby satisfying the moral law. The second part of the Law—types and shadows—addresses the issue of man's failure at keeping the moral law.

Types and shadows

The second part of the Law included detailed instructions concerning temple sacrifices, feast days and ceremonial worship. These laws—including the making of sacrifices, the placement of furniture in the temple, the observance of feast days and others were types and shadows foretelling the ultimate solution to man's dilemma.

Because it was impossible for the Law to be accomplished by man, it was constantly being broken. As a result, a system of sacrifices was established to be offered to atone or cover for man's failure to fulfill the Law. While the sacrifices and observances were established to deal with the failures of man in Old Testament life, these sacrifices and observances were also a shadow of Jesus, the ultimate sacrifice and solution to man's sin. Under this system, every time a sacrifice was made for sin, it pointed to the coming of Jesus the Messiah who would put away sin and its power forever. Hebrews 10:1–4 declares this fact:

> For the law, having a shadow of the good things to come, and not the very image of the things, can never with these same sacrifices, which they offer continually year by year, make those who approach perfect. For then would they not have ceased to be offered? For the worshipers, once purified, would have had no more consciousness of sins. But in those sacrifices there is a reminder of sins every year. For it is not possible that the blood of bulls and goats could take away sins.

The early sacrifices had no power to remove permanently the acts of sin, or the sin nature. On the contrary, these offerings only served as a reminder to the people of their sinfulness and their need for a Savior.

In his book *The Spirit-Controlled Life*, Bob Yandian states this point clearly, saying:

> This system was just a shadow of the real sacrifice, which was yet to come. The ritualistic elements of Jewish worship all had a meaning. They symbolized the death, burial and resurrection of the promised Messiah, the Savior of Israel, the Lord Jesus Christ. Whether the worship ritual involved a grain offering, an offering of wine or oil, the

bringing of the firstfruits to the altar, or the blood sacrifice of a dove, lamb or oxen, it always portrayed one thing: the atonement, the sacrifice of the life of the Savior for His people. Thus the whole ceremonial system evolved around and centered on blood. Why? To continually remind the people of the blood of the Anointed One, which would be shed for the remission of their sins.[1]

Thus, from the giving of the Law to Moses, we see God leading us to an awareness of our inability to keep His standards and to the recognition, through His types and shadows, of His ultimate solution to our sin problem in the gift of His own Son, Jesus, as our ultimate sacrifice.

Social law

The third part of the law established regulations and instructions concerning the proper care of lands and crops. It also dealt with dietary regulations and with instructions concerning what was clean and unclean.

We shall see, as we study God's Word about the Law, that both the moral law and the social law were fulfilled by the perfect life of Christ. We can also see, through the types and shadows of the law, the perfect fulfillment of Jesus by His death and resurrection.

THE NATURE OF THE LAW

In order to understand the nature and the purpose of the Law, it is important to realize that the Law was given specifically to Israel. In Exodus 19:3 we read, "And Moses went up to God, and the LORD called to him from the mountain, saying, 'Thus you shall say to the house of Jacob, and tell the children of Israel.'" Leviticus 26:46 says, "These are the statutes and judgments and laws which the LORD made between Himself and the children of Israel on Mount Sinai by the hand of Moses."

The point is, if the Law was given specifically to the children of Israel, then it would stand to reason that the Law does not apply to the Gentiles. The apostle Paul makes the following statement in Romans 2:12: "For as many as have sinned without law will also perish without law, and as many as have sinned in the law will be judged by the law." In verse 14 Paul goes on to say, "For when Gentiles, who do not have the law, by nature do the things in the law, these, although not having the law, are a law to themselves."

Therefore, the Gentiles were never subject to the Jewish law for two reasons. First, it was not given to the Gentiles—it was given to Israel. Second, Jesus in His life, death and resurrection fulfilled the Law and all of its requirements.

Now, it is true that the principles of the Law, particularly those in the moral law, apply to mankind as a whole. Yet the requirements within the Law could never be fulfilled by man. It is literally impossible for anyone in their own goodness or strength to fulfill the requirements of the Law. The good news is that it is not up to us to fulfill the righteous requirements of the Law. They have already been fulfilled through the death, burial and resurrection of Jesus Christ. This is not to say that we do not have an obligation to live godly and holy lives. But our righteousness, our justification before God, is not based on what we do or don't do. It is based on what Jesus did two thousand years ago.

The Law, made up of outward regulations, set a standard of holiness that called for a life of flawless perfection. It was a standard that was good, yet it was a standard that could never be met. Why? Because the weakness of the Law was in the flesh. By that I mean that the nature of the Law, with its regulations and rules, left the fulfillment of the Law in the hands of man. Man in the weakness of his flesh could never meet the perfect standard that the Law required.

Paul the Apostle speaks of this in Romans 7:5 when he says, "For when we were in the flesh, the sinful passions which were aroused by the law were at work in our members [the flesh] to bear fruit to death." In setting the standard of perfection, the Law, because of its nature of rules, ignited the weakness and passions of the flesh, making it clear to man that he is sinful and incapable of fulfilling the requirements of the Law.

As a result, man under the Law was left with a sense of guilt and consciousness of sin. The apostle Paul writes in Romans 7:8–11, saying, "But sin, taking opportunity by the commandment, produced in me all manner of evil desire. For apart from the law sin was dead. I was alive once without the law, but when the commandment came, sin revived and I died. And the commandment, which was to bring life, I found to bring death. For sin, taking occasion by the commandment, deceived me, and by it killed me."

It wasn't that the Law was evil. On the contrary, the Law was established by God, and it was good. The problem lay in the fact that the righteous requirement of the Law exposed the passions of sin that resided in the flesh of man. Paul said it in the following way:

> Has then what is good become death to me? Certainly not! But sin, that it might appear sin, was producing death in me through what is good [the Law], so that sin through the commandment might become exceedingly sinful. For we know that the law is spiritual, but I am carnal, sold under sin.
> —ROMANS 7:13–14

Paul's struggle was not with the inward man. Notice what he says in Romans 7:22–24:

> For I delight in the law of God according to the inward man. But I see another law in my members [the flesh], warring against the law my mind [the soul], and bringing me into captivity to the law of sin which is in my members. O wretched man that I am! Who will deliver me from this body of death?

Had Paul stayed under the rule of the Law, he would have continued to find himself in a place of sin consciousness. *He would have continued to suffer under the torment of shame and fear regarding his sinfulness—the same fear and shame that drove Adam and Eve to hide from the presence of God.*

Isaiah was a man under the Law, a man under the Old Covenant, who was brought to a moment in time when he realized his inadequacy and sin in the light of God's holiness. After seeing the holiness and majesty of God, he cried out:

Woe is me, for I am undone! Because I am a man of unclean lips, and I dwell in the midst of a people of unclean lips; for my eyes have seen the King, the Lord of Hosts.

—Isaiah 6:5

Under the Old Covenant, God established offerings and sacrifices that would bring forgiveness for the acts of sin committed by the people of Israel. These offerings were meant to testify of the ultimate offering of God's Son, whose blood carried more power than the blood of goats and bulls. The blood of the animal sacrifices could only atone for the outward acts of sin. The blood of Jesus, on the other hand, carries power to purge a man's conscience and to cleanse him from the inside out. In other words, the blood shed by the sacrifices under the Old Covenant offered forgiveness for the deeds of sin as well as for the consequent sense of guilt. However, the blood of Jesus set us free not only from the guilt of sin, but it also delivers us from the power of sin.

Notice what the writer of Hebrews says about the blood of Jesus:

For if the blood of bulls and goats and the ashes of a heifer, sprinkling the unclean, sanctifies for the purifying of the flesh, how much more shall the blood of Christ, who through the eternal Spirit offered Himself without spot to God, cleanse your conscience from dead works to serve the living God?

—Hebrews 9:13–14

164

A Child of the Law or a Son of Love?

Thank God for the blood of Jesus! Through the blood of Jesus our conscience is purged from a sense of guilt and condemnation. Our conscience is purged from a sense of fear that God has forsaken us because of our sins. The same blood that purges us from a sense of guilt, shame and fear is also able to empower us to live for God in true holiness. Yet, Isaiah was overwhelmed by his sin and the sin of Israel—as well he should have been! His encounter with the holiness and majesty of God occurred before the sacrifice of Jesus, the finished work of Christ.

Is man any more holy now than when Isaiah encountered God? Not necessarily. But today, this Law that declared us all sinners has been fulfilled by Christ. There is no more penalty for sin. The penalty of sin was death, but that penalty has been paid through the death of Christ. In addition, when Jesus raised Himself from the dead, He defeated death. Not only was the power of death itself destroyed, but Jesus redeemed man from the fear of death that had tormented him from the time of the Fall of man in the garden.

It is not God's desire for us to continue in a consciousness of sin. This celebrates man and his weakness and the human nature. Sin consciousness imprisons man in fear and shame. Rather, God's desire is that we be conscious of the finished work of Christ and His righteousness that has been imputed to everyone who places their trust in Him to be justified instead of trusting that we are made just by what we do. True holiness is not achieved by focusing our energies and thoughts on our sin, but rather by celebrating the power of the cross and our righteousness that is found in Him, the Righteous One.

The apostle Paul wrote to the Philippian believers:

> That I may…be found in Him, not having my own righteousness, which is from the law, but that which is through faith in Christ, the righteousness which is from God by faith.
> —PHILIPPIANS 3:8–9

Paul goes on to say it was by celebrating this righteousness that he would be able to know Jesus intimately, to know the power of His resurrection and the fellowship of Christ's sufferings, and eventually to be conformed to His death (v. 10).

In Galatians 2:16 we read, "Knowing that a man is not justified by the works of the law but by faith in Jesus Christ, even we have believed in Christ Jesus, that we might be justified by faith in Christ and not by the works of the law; for by the works of the law no flesh shall be justified."

THE PURPOSE OF THE LAW

Seeing that the sacrifices made under the Old Covenant testified of the coming of Jesus, and that it is the finished work of Christ that justifies, what then was the purpose of the Law?

In Galatians 3:21–23 Paul explains the purpose of the Law:

> Is the law then against the promises of God? Certainly not! For if there had been a law given which could have given life, truly righteousness would have been by the law. But the Scripture has

confined all under sin, that the promise by faith in
Jesus Christ might be given to those who believe.
But before faith came, we were kept under guard by
the law, kept for the faith which would afterward be
revealed.

The Scripture says that before faith came—or in other
words, before Jesus came to redeem mankind—we were
kept under the guard of the Law. Notice that Paul goes
on to say that the Law was our tutor (v. 24). The Greek
word for *tutor* is *paidagogas*. The first part of this word is
taken from the word *pais*, which is interpreted as "child."
The second part of the word is *agogas*, which is the
English word for "leader." The King James Bible translates the word *tutor* as "schoolmaster."

The idea is that the Law was to function in mankind in
the same way that an instructor teaches a child. Just as
there is a time when the instructor is no longer needed as
the child grows to adulthood, the Law was no longer
needed after Christ came and redeemed mankind. In his
letter to the Galatians, Paul put it this way: "But after faith
has come, we are no longer under a tutor. For you are all
sons of God through faith in Christ Jesus" (Gal. 3:25–26).

Paul further expands our understanding in the first
verse of the fourth chapter of Galatians.

Now I say that the heir, as long as he is a child, does
not differ at all from a slave, though he is master of
all, but is under guardians and stewards until the
time appointed by the father.

The analogy is clear. A child of the master is heir of all

the master possesses. But he is unable to walk in the strength and fullness of his inheritance, with all of its privileges and power, while he is a child. During his years of adolescence, he is under the charge and rule of a guardian. The task of the guardian is to teach the child in such a way that he prepares him and points him toward his destiny. It is also the task of the guardian to discipline the child if he oversteps the boundaries established by his father, the master.

This tutelage continues until the appointed time by the father—the time when the father deems the child mature enough to handle the responsibilities, privileges and power of his inheritance. When that time arrives, the guardian's task is over. His services are no longer needed, and his job is obsolete.

This is a perfect description of the task of the Law. Look at what Paul writes in Galatians 4:3:

> Even so we, when we were children, were in bondage under the elements of the world. But when the fullness of the time had come, God sent forth His Son, born of a woman, born under the law, to redeem those who were under the law, that we might receive the adoption as sons.

Before Jesus came, we too were like children in need of a schoolmaster. The Law was a guardian to instruct mankind and to bring discipline. But it does more. Just as a guardian is to point the child of the master to his destiny, in the same way the Law was to point us to our destiny—becoming mature sons and daughters in Jesus.

What was Paul saying to the churches in Galatia? He

was saying that if they allowed themselves to be brought back under the Law, they would be reverting back to the place of children in need of a tutor or guardian. They would be relinquishing their sonship—and its privileges. But more importantly, they would be relinquishing the *power* to live as sons. In Paul's mind, doing so would lower their way of living.

When Jesus redeemed man, the purpose of the Law became obsolete. I am not saying that the Law was destroyed. The Law wasn't destroyed—rather it was fulfilled in Jesus. Because of the finished work of Jesus, the Law is no longer necessary. Living as sons and daughters of God is a higher way to live.

Galatians 4:6–7 tells us why living as sons instead of as children is so powerful.

> And because you are sons, God has sent forth the Spirit of His Son into your hearts, crying out, "Abba, Father!" Therefore you are no longer a slave but a son, and if a son, then an heir of God through Christ.

Children relate to their father differently than do mature sons and daughters. Even though we are always the children of our parents, as we reach adulthood, our relationship changes. We are able to communicate with our parents on a different level than can a preschooler or a teenager. As adults, our potential for a rich relationship with our parents is greater. This point is exactly what Paul was trying to get across to the churches in Galatia. We no longer need to relate to God through the Law. Because of Jesus, we are no longer slaves. Therefore we have the opportunity to relate to God as full heirs through Christ. With the Law obsolete through the sacrifice of Jesus, each believer is able to experience the power of the Spirit.

THE POWER OF THE SPIRIT

Bonnie and I had just finished teaching at a marriage conference with another couple in Breckenridge, Colorado. Bonnie rode back home to Colorado Springs with the couple with whom we held the marriage conference, and I drove on to Greeley. I arrived at the motel early that Saturday afternoon. As I sat in the room, I began to read the Book of Galatians. I had been spending some time meditating on certain passages from Galatians. As I read the third chapter of Galatians that afternoon, a powerful truth dawned on me. Galatians 3:13–14 says:

> Christ has redeemed us from the curse of the law, having become a curse for us (for it is written, "Cursed is everyone who hangs on a tree"), that the blessing of Abraham might come upon the Gentiles in Christ Jesus, that we might receive the promise of the Spirit through faith.

I had read those verses many times and never really noticed the progression of truth found in them. I believe that these two verses capsulize the entire theme of Paul's letter. Most people believe that the main point of Galatians is to show the contrast between the Law and grace. Even though the contrast between Law and grace is a dominant theme in this book, it is not the main point.

Look carefully at the progression of these two verses.

1. "Christ has redeemed us from the curse of the law…"

We have thoroughly discussed the fact and the result of Christ's redemption of mankind in the earlier pages of this chapter.

2. "…that the blessing of Abraham might come upon the Gentiles in Christ Jesus…"

The next step of the progression is that all who have been redeemed from the curse of the Law may be partakers of the blessing of Abraham (v. 14). This blessing, which is found in Deuteronomy 28:1–14, is wonderful, but even this is not the main point of Paul's progression.

3. "…that we might receive the promise of the Spirit through faith."

This is the main point. We can receive the promise of the Spirit.

This was the main issue for Paul. The contrast made between the Law and grace was necessary to show the churches in Galatia that if they went back under the Law, they would return to a place of infancy, which would polarize them from the power and life of the Spirit. The Law had its limitations. For example, the Law could not produce miracles. Miracles were a result of the work of the Spirit. Notice what Paul says in Galatians 3:5, "Therefore He who supplies the Spirit to you and works miracles among you, does He do it by the works of the law, or by the hearing of faith?" No doubt, as Paul preached the good news of the gospel, there were miracles of healing and deliverance that took place. The believers in Galatia witnessed the miracle-working power of the Spirit. Paul knew that these miracles didn't happen by the Law—they were a work of the Spirit.

It wasn't the Law that supplied them with the tangible working of the Spirit. It was faith in Christ that released the power of the Spirit's working. In Galatians 3:2, Paul says, "This only I want to learn from you: Did you receive the Spirit by the works of the law, or by the hearing of faith?" Why was this so important to Paul? Because Paul knew that without the working of the Spirit in their lives, they would be slaves to their flesh and emotions— including shame, guilt and, more importantly, fear.

THE LIBERTY OF THE SPIRIT

In Galatians 5:1 we read, "Stand fast therefore in the liberty by which Christ has made us free, and do not be entangled again with a yoke of bondage." The word *liberty* is the Greek word *eleutheria*. The definition of this word does not refer to a liberty that represents the kind of life a person lives. It is not the kind of liberty that gives man license to behave in any manner in which he sees fit. The liberty that Paul is talking about is the *method* by which one lives life.

According to Paul, under the Law a person has no more liberty than a child has under the care and authority of a guardian. Anyone who counts on the observance of the Law to justify him or her before God is like an adult who puts himself under rules made for children. If the Galatians had submitted themselves to circumcision, they

172

would be putting themselves under the Law and therefore depriving themselves of the ministry of the Holy Spirit, which is not provided under the Law. In the same way, anytime we place our trust in something other than Jesus to make us just before God, we too return back to the place of children, hindering the work and power of the Holy Spirit in our lives.

The Spirit not only produces miracles, but He also produces the greatest spiritual force known to man—the spiritual force of love.

> The fruit of the Spirit is love, joy, peace, longsuf-fering, kindness, goodness, faithfulness, gentleness, self-control. Against such there is no law.
> —GALATIANS 5:22–23

Notice that this verse doesn't say the *fruits* of the Spirit—it says the *fruit* of the Spirit. The rest of the verse contains the attributes of love.

In the beginning of this chapter I stated that the Law empowers fear in man, because the Law celebrates the weakness and sinfulness of man. The Law polarizes man from the power of the Holy Spirit in his life, who produces the force of love—the ultimate cure for fear.

As long as you and I attempt to justify ourselves before God by what we do, we will continue to live under the weight of the Law. Consequently, we will open our lives up to fear. Fear that God has forsaken us. Fear that He is punishing us for our sins, or has abandoned us because of our transgressions. Yet, as we embrace His grace over our lives, we are open to the power of His Spirit and to the fruit of His love.

Chapter 11

THE FORCE OF LOVE

O*ne day Jesus* was teaching when He noticed a commotion near the back of the crowd. As He turned his attention toward the direction of the noise, He saw the crowd begin to part, making way for three men and a woman. As they approached the front of the crowd, one of the men violently shoved the woman forward as he announced her identity by yelling out, "Whore!" She slid several feet from the force, ending face down in a cloud of dust just inches from the Master's feet. She slowly gathered herself, pulling herself up to her knees. You could hear a few teeters of nervous laughter, but most people of the crowd were silent.

For the first few seconds, Jesus was able to see her face. When their eyes met, she quickly dropped her head and stared blankly at the ground. Her heavy makeup was spotted by smudges of dirt. The smell of cheap perfume mixed with sweat was unmistakably a result of her recent activity. Wet strands of hair hung in her face, and her eyes were framed by long dark lashes. She was partially covered by a sheet, which was all she had the time to grab as she was snatched from her bedroom of secrets.

"The Law says she must die!" one of the men spat.

"What do You say?" another asked defiantly. The crowd began to press in closer, forming a tight circle. Every eye was on the Master. Jesus looked directly at the obvious ringleader, His eyes narrowing with anger. The thirty or so seconds of silence that passed seemed an eternity. Finally, Jesus took a deep breath and said, "Anyone here…I mean, *anyone* who has never sinned…throw the first stone to her head." Then Jesus lowered Himself to His knees, facing the woman, and with His finger wrote in the dust on the ground. Several moments passed.

The scarlet woman squeezed her eyes tightly shut as she waited for the merciless strike of the first stone. All at once she heard a thud…then another…and another as rocks dropped systematically to the earth. As she opened her eyes, she saw Jesus kneeling in front of her. Looking around, she realized they were the only two people left. Everyone else had gone.

She braced herself, not knowing what to expect next. "Is there no one left to condemn you?" Jesus asked.

"No…I guess not," she nervously muttered.

The Force of Love

"Well then, neither do I condemn you," Jesus responded. "You're free to go."

The woman slowly rose to her feet and turned to leave, but Jesus continued speaking. "As you go," He said, "I want you to know that you are worth much more than this." He dropped two copper coins to the ground. She understood exactly what He meant.

This story is a powerful example of the love of God. God's love is the greatest force in the universe. Yet many still know little about it, and even fewer have ever really experienced the impact of His love.

The subject of love has intrigued man since the beginning. There has never been a single subject that has had more songs sung about it or stories woven around it. Yet with all of the songs and stories and thought put into it, a revelation of God's love seems to elude the hearts of many.

There are four words in the Greek for love. The first one is the Greek word *eros*. This is where we get our English word *erotic*. This word is used to describe the sexual desire between man and woman. This word was thought to carry the idea of the basest expression of human affection—purely physical and completely self-centered. The early Christians were unable to use this word at all; therefore, it does not appear in a single place in the New Testament.

The second word for love in the Greek language is the word *storge*. This word was used most commonly to describe the affection you see between family members. It has also been used to describe the love someone may have for their country or for a leader. It was used to describe the love parents have toward their children and that children have toward their parents. In Romans 12:10, the apostle Paul writes, "Be kindly affectionate to one another with brotherly love, in honor giving preference to one another." The phrase "kindly affectionate" uses the Greek adjective *philostorgos*, which refers to the affection that is present between parents and their children. I like the use of this word because it strongly implies that in Paul's mind, the Christian community is not a society, nor an army, but a family.

The third Greek word for love is *phileo*. It is the most common word for love used in the Greek language. It is best translated as *cherish*. It is used to describe the love a husband has for his wife. It can also be used to describe the strong affection between friends. It is a deeper affection than what the word *storge* can describe. For example, in John 11:3 we read, "Therefore the sisters sent to Him, saying, 'Lord, behold, he whom You love is sick.'" The sisters to which this verse refers are the sisters of Lazarus, and they were informing Jesus that Lazarus was dying. The word *love* in this verse is the word *phileo*. It is the strongest word the Greeks had to communicate a passion that went beyond the physical, as well as transcending concern for one's self.

In John 20:2, we see this word used again, this time describing the love Jesus had for the apostle John:

> Then she ran and came to Simon Peter, and to the other disciple, *whom Jesus loved*, and said to them, "They have taken away the Lord out of the tomb, and we do not know where they have laid Him."
>
> —EMPHASIS ADDED

The Force of Love

There are other times when the word *phileo* is used in the New Testament. For example, in John 5:20 we read, "For the Father loves the Son, and shows Him all things that He Himself does; and He will show Him greater works than these, that you may marvel." The word for *love* in this verse is *phileo*. In John 16:27 Jesus spoke of the Father's love for mankind by saying, "For the Father Himself loves you, because you have loved Me, and have believed that I came forth from God." The word *loves* again is the word *phileo*. In 1 Corinthians 16:22, when the apostle Paul speaks of the *love* that we are to have for Jesus, he uses the word *phileo*.

The word *phileo*, as we have seen, is a wonderful word and expresses genuine warmth and affection. Why wasn't this word good enough, then, for the early Christians? Because the word *phileo* was really meant to be used to describe a deep affection felt toward those near to us—a child, a parent, relatives and close friends. The early church needed a word that was more inclusive. They needed a word that expressed the same depth of affection, yet that was extended to the entire world—including one's enemies.

This brings us to the fourth word for *love* in the Greek language. The fourth, and by far the most common, word used for *love* in the Greek is the word *agape*. The noun *agape* appears in the New Testament nearly one hundred twenty times, and the adjective *agapan* is used more than one hundred thirty times.[1]

Agape is best described as God's kind of love. All the other words for love express emotion. God's love has to do with the mind. It is not an emotion that is always felt,

179

but rather it is a principle by which we deliberately live. Therefore, God's love has to do with the will. God's kind of love, when necessary, will exercise conquest and victory over the emotions. For example, we are commanded by God to love our enemies. Yet no one would ever naturally love his enemies. But in God's love we can. God's love has the ability to conquer all of our natural inclinations and emotions.

Jesus spoke of this *agape* love by saying:

> You have heard that it was said, "An eye for an eye and a tooth for a tooth." But I tell you not to resist an evil person. But whoever slaps you on your right cheek, turn the other to him also. If anyone wants to sue you and take away your tunic, let him have your cloak also....You have heard that it was said, "You shall love your neighbor and hate your enemy." But I say to you, love your enemies, bless those who curse you, do good to those who hate you, and pray for those who spitefully use you and persecute you, that you may be sons of your Father in heaven; for He makes His sun rise on the evil and on the good, and sends rain on the just and the unjust. For if you love those who love you, what reward have you? Do not even the tax collectors do the same? And if you greet your brethren only, what do you do more than others? Do not even the tax collectors do so? Therefore you shall be perfect, just as your Father in heaven is perfect.
> —MATTHEW 5:38–40, 43–48

Jesus would never command us to do something that

180

He has not given us the grace to accomplish. God commands us to love—no matter what. Yet there is a grace found within His love for us that empowers us to love others. God's love is not void of emotion, but it does transcend them. God's love does not take its orders (how it will feel and what it will do) from the emotional realm of man, but rather God's love dictates to the will the choice to love regardless of feeling. The "feelings" of love will always follow the choice to love.

The same is true with God's love for us. God's love has nothing to do with us. God's love has to do with God—independent of our actions. It is not based on us or on our performance.

That is why Jesus responded to the woman caught in adultery in the way He did. He wasn't defending or justifying her actions. The mercy He extended to her was independent of her sin. Jesus knew that love was a greater conquering force than judgment. Jesus knew that the fears and conflicts that caused this woman to think she could find happiness in her sin would be vanquished by the force of unconditional love.

The love of God always seeks the highest good for man, regardless of man's state of sin. Why? Because God's love is not subject to our sins. We can't do anything to alter or change His love for us. No matter what we do, He would never love us any less. Nor can we do anything to cause God to love us any more than He does. It is a settled issue in the heart of God, one which will never change—not one iota. Even the laws of the universe declare God's unconditional love for us. Note again the words of Matthew 5:44–45:

> But I say to you, love your enemies, bless those who
> curse you, do good to those who hate you, and pray
> for those who spitefully use you and persecute you,
> that you may be sons of your Father in heaven; for
> He makes His sun rise on the evil and on the good,
> and sends rain on the just and on the unjust.

It is not the good and the moral who receive the warmth of the sun and the evil who receive the lightning and thunder clouds of rain. When it comes to His love, it is impossible for God to show partiality based on how we live our lives. This is certainly not a justification for man to sin. Nor does this fact express how God views the seriousness of man's sin, except to say that it does not change God's love toward the sinner. Regardless of our sin, He still loves us.

In 1 John 4:17–18 we read:

> Love has been perfected among us in this: that we
> may have boldness in the day of judgment; because
> as He is, so are we in this world. There is no fear in
> love; but perfect love casts out fear, because fear
> involves torment. But he who fears has not been
> made perfect in love.

It is clear that fear involves torment. We have certainly seen this fact within the pages of this book. I am sure that many of you have known firsthand the torment that fear brings. It is God's perfect love that drives out all fear. It is as we discover His love for us that we are able to live free from the tormenting fears of life. Look at Ephesians 3:17–21.

That Christ may dwell in your hearts through faith; that you, being rooted and grounded in love, may be able to comprehend with all the saints what is the width and length and depth and height—to know the love of Christ which passes knowledge; that you may be filled with all the fullness of God. Now to Him who is able to do exceedingly abundantly above all that we ask or think, according to the power that works in us, to Him be glory in the church by Christ Jesus to all generations, forever and ever.

Notice the apostle Paul said that we were to be rooted and grounded in the love of God. According to Paul, as we are deeply established in the revelation of God's love for us, it is then we begin to experience His fullness in our lives.

When I read this verse I can't help but think of the Sears Tower in Chicago. The Sears Tower is one of the tallest buildings in the world. The two antennas at the top of the superstructure raise the points of the tower 1,700 feet into the air, 110 stories above Chicago's sidewalks. More important is the foundation of this massive building. The building's foundation consists of 114 steel-shelled cassions spaced 15 feet apart. Each cassion supports one column of the tower. Remarkably, each cassion descends 100 feet into the earth, embedded deep into the limestone bedrock. It took three years to build, but eighteen months of that time were dedicated to the laying of the foundation. Why? Because the foundation is the most important part of any building. If it wasn't for the stability of the foundation, it wouldn't take long for the rest of the structure to collapse under the stress of high winds.

The same is true for us. It is the foundation of God's love that enables us to live out the superstructure of His blessings in our lives. His love reinforces us, stabilizing us against the stormy winds of life.

THE POWER OF GOD'S LOVE

Let's look at some power points concerning the love of God.

Love is the very nature of God.

> Finally, brethren, farewell. Become complete. Be of good comfort, be of one mind, live in peace; and the *God of love* and peace will be with you.
> —2 CORINTHIANS 13:11, EMPHASIS ADDED

> And we have known and believed the love that God has for us. *God is love*, and he who abides in love abides in God, and God in him.
> —1 JOHN 4:16, EMPHASIS ADDED

God's love isn't something that *He does*; it is *who He is*. He *is* love. It is a part of His very nature. Consequently, it would be impossible for you to change His love for you. That would equate with changing God's very nature.

God's love is universal.

It was not only the chosen nation of Israel that God loved, but the world. Everyone and anyone who comes to Him, He will in no way cast out. There is no sin that a man or woman can commit that disqualifies them from the love and salvation of God. "For God so loved the world…"

God's love is a sacrificial love.

God's love is a giving love. The proof of God's unconditional love is the fact that He was willing to give His life for those who could never earn or deserve it. First John 3:16 says, "By this we know love, because He laid down His life for us. And we also ought to lay down our lives for the brethren." What was the proof of His love for us? The love Jesus has for us wasn't defined as an emotion or a sense of sentiment; it was defined by the fact that He did something. He laid down His life for us.

The apostle Paul declared, "I have been crucified with Christ; it is no longer I who live, but Christ lives in me; and the life which I now live in the flesh, I live by faith in the Son of God, *who loved me and gave Himself for me*" (Gal. 2:20, emphasis added). In Ephesians 5:2 we read, "And walk in love, as Christ also has loved us and given Himself for us, an offering and a sacrifice to God for a sweet-smelling aroma." God gave Himself to us as the ultimate gift and expression of love. His love is truly sacrificial.

God's love is undeserved.

When we had nothing to offer God, He loved us and died for us. Romans 5:8 says, "But God demonstrates His own love toward us, in that *while we were still sinners,* Christ died for us" (emphasis added). Even after we come to Him in faith, we are still undeserving of His goodness and mercy. You need not fear that you have done anything to cause God to withdraw His love from you.

God's love is a sanctifying love.

Second Thessalonians 2:13 says, "…because God from the beginning chose you for salvation through sanctification by the Spirit and belief in the truth." Love is the fruit of the Spirit, and it is the Spirit's work through love that accomplishes that sanctifying work. The word *sanctification* in the Greek is the word *hagiasmos*, from which we get our English word for *holiness*. God's love purifies our hearts, washing them free from selfish desires and impure motives.

God's love produces conquerors.

Romans 8:37 reads, "Yet in all these things we are more than conquerors through Him who loved us." The love of God replaces fear with courage and timidity with boldness. When we are confident in God's love and goodness, then we can face our enemies with an assurance of victory. We know that God, who seeks our highest good, would never allow evil to triumph over us.

God's love is inseparable.

Since God's love is unconditional, then there is nothing we can do to change His heart toward us. There is also nothing life can do to separate us from His love for us.

> Who shall separate us from the love of Christ? Shall tribulation, or distress, or persecution, or famine, or

186

nakedness, or peril, or sword?....For I am per-
suaded that neither death nor life, nor angels nor
principalities nor powers, nor things present nor
things to come, nor height nor depth, nor any other
created thing, shall be able to separate us from the
love of God which is in Christ Jesus our Lord.
—ROMANS 8:35, 38–39

God's love is an obedient love.

According to the Scriptures, obedience is the final
proof of love. It was the love of Jesus toward the Father
that caused Him to lay down His life in obedience. Jesus
said, "I can of Myself do nothing. As I hear, I judge; and
My judgment is righteous, because I do not seek My
own will but the will of the Father who sent Me" (John
5:30). In the same way, our obedience is proof of our
love for God. In John 14:15 Jesus said, "If you love Me,
keep My commandments." Jesus went on to say, "If
anyone loves Me, he will keep My word" (v. 23).

God's love is sincere.

God's love is pure and honest—void of any ulterior
motives or hidden agendas.

… by purity, by knowledge, by longsuffering, by
kindness, by the Holy Spirit, by *sincere* love.
—2 CORINTHIANS 6:6, EMPHASIS ADDED

Since you have purified your souls in obeying the
truth through the Spirit in sincere love of the brethren, love one another fervently with a pure heart.
—1 PETER 1:22

187

God's only agenda is to change us through His love. In the same way we also are commanded to love others with the same sincerity of heart.

God's love empowers faith.

Love is the force behind faith. If we are convinced that God loves us, then we are sure that we can trust Him with every area of our lives. This, in its simplicity, is faith. We expend so much energy trying to believe God, trying to increase our faith in Him. This is the most unscriptural approach to a relationship with God that I have ever heard. A small child doesn't try to believe his or her parents. A child simply believes. The apostle Paul speaks of this truth in his letter to the Galatians, saying, "For in Christ Jesus neither circumcision nor uncircumcison avails anything, but faith working through love" (Gal. 5:6).

PURSUE LOVE

The ultimate cure for fear is the perfect love of God. As we surrender our hearts and dare to embrace His love for us, our fears lose their hold over our hearts. Mentally accepting the fact that God loves us unconditionally is not enough. To know—to experience His love—brings the revelation necessary to drive fear out of our lives. Anything of value must be pursued. This includes a revelation of the love of God. For example, the apostle Paul writes, "And now abide faith, hope, love, these three; but the greatest of these is love. Pursue love…" (1 Cor. 13:13–14:1).

In 2 Thessalonians 3:5 Paul writes:

The Force of Love

> Now may the Lord direct your hearts into the love
> of God and into the patience of Christ.

You and I must choose to pursue a revelation of God's love. Please, don't misunderstand; you are not asking God to love you more than He already loves you—you are asking for a greater revelation of His love, which, in its fullness, has already been placed upon you. We must direct our hearts toward love. We need to meditate on the scriptures that declare His wonderful love for us, and we must translate that love to others.

As we do, the fears that have tormented us will, bit by bit, loose their hold over our hearts.

Why?

Because there is no room for fear in the presence of love!

Chapter 12

THE FEAR OF GOD

I *have dedicated the* entire book thus far to the subject of unhealthy fear. Yet, there are several times where we see fear used in a positive sense. For example, in Matthew 10:28 Jesus instructs us in what we should fear, saying:

> And do not fear those who kill the body but cannot kill the soul. But rather fear Him who is able to destroy both soul and body in hell.

Here Jesus warns us that we have no need to fear those who have the power to take away our physical life. Those who are born again simply go on to the presence of the Lord when physical life comes to an end for whatever reason. The apostle Paul, when speaking of the possibility of his death, said, "We are confident, yes, well pleased rather to be absent from the body and to be present with the Lord" (2 Cor. 5:8).

Jesus said that we are not to fear those who have the power to end our physical lives. But, because all mankind will spend eternity somewhere—either in heaven or in hell—Jesus said we were to fear Him who can destroy our physical life as well as our soul. To whom is Jesus making reference? To God—who has the control over a man's final destiny—and the power to destroy both soul and body in hell.

Since God has the power to destroy both soul and body in hell, what type of fear, then, are we to demonstrate toward Satan? It is obvious that this type of fear is not the same fear—or reverence—that we show toward God. The fear we are to have toward Satan is a sobering realization of the power of Satan's deception and his desire for our ultimate destruction. This fear is meant to cause us to take seriously the intentions of our enemy and to maintain a sense of dependence, surrender and trust in Jesus as our safeguard.

Therefore, along with understanding the seriousness concerning Satan's desire to destroy man's soul, we are also commanded to fear God. As we allow Him to capture our hearts and affections, we discover His power against our enemy.

THE BLESSINGS OF FEARING GOD

There are several Scriptures in the Old and New Testaments where we are commanded to fear God. Many verses describe the benefits of demonstrating the fear of the Lord by the way we live and relate to God. The Book of Proverbs describes many of the benefits of fearing God. Let's take a look at some of these benefits.

Wisdom

In Proverbs 1:7 we read that fearing God is the beginning of knowledge. In Proverbs 9:10 we read, "The fear of the LORD is the beginning of wisdom, and the knowledge of the Holy One is understanding."

According to these scriptures, as we choose to fear God we are able to operate by His wisdom and knowledge. There are many Christians who trust their own intellect to get them through life. Our own intellects will never be enough to give us the wisdom to make the important decisions of our lives. But we can walk in wisdom if we will humble ourselves and fear God. His wisdom operating through our lives will give us the confidence to face life's decisions.

Life

Fearing God brings life. In Proverbs 19:23 we read, "The fear of the LORD leads to life, and he who has it [the fear of God] will abide in satisfaction; he will not be visited by evil."

The fear of God places us on the pathway of life. It keeps us on the path and prevents us from falling into pitfalls along the way. Proverbs 14:27 says, "The fear of the LORD is a fountain of life, to turn one away from the snares of death."

Through His resurrection, Christ has already provided us with all things that pertain to life and godliness

(2 Pet. 1:3). Even so, many still struggle in defeat with the issues of life. The reason is that they, through stubbornness, insist on being the lord of their own lives. It is the fear of God that places us on that path to experience His life and peace.

Confidence against our adversaries

In Proverbs 14:26 we read, "In the fear of the LORD there is strong confidence, and His children will have a place of refuge." We find confidence in the time of adversity through our fear of the Lord. Our fear of God empowers us to see the place of refuge that we have in Him during tribulation. If we fear God, then we will not fear what man can do to us. As a matter of fact, it is impossible to fear God and at the same time struggle with a fear of man. There is a direct correlation between that in which we choose to place our fear and our response to times of adversity. Either we will fear God, or we will fear man. If we allow our hearts to be overwhelmed by the fear of man, then we will be blinded from seeing the place of refuge we have in our God.

A MISCONCEPTION CONCERNING THE FEAR OF GOD

Over the years there has been a gross misconception concerning the fear of God. This misconception has been perpetuated by the misinterpretation of the first five verses of the sixth chapter of Isaiah:

> In the year that King Uzziah died, I saw the Lord sitting on a throne, high and lifted up, and the train

of His robe filled the temple. Above it stood seraphim; each one had six wings: with two he covered his face, with two he covered his feet, and with two he flew. And he cried to another and said: "Holy holy, holy is the Lord of hosts; the whole earth is full of His glory!" And the posts of the door were shaken by the voice of him who cried out, and the house was filled with smoke. So I said, "Woe is me, for I am undone! Because I am a man of unclean lips, and I dwell in the midst of a people of unclean lips; for my eyes have seen the King, the Lord of hosts."

—Isaiah 6:1–5

In chapter ten I mentioned that over the years I have heard many preachers quote this passage as an example of what our response should be in the light of the manifest presence of God. Many teach that if we truly have the fear of God in our hearts, we should respond to the presence of God in the same way that Isaiah did—by writhing in our own sense of sinfulness in the light of His holiness. For many in the church at large, this interpretation is taught as an example of what it means to possess a fear of the Lord.

For a Christian, however, this response is unscriptural. A response like Isaiah's would be appropriate for a nonbeliever who suddenly becomes aware of the presence of a holy God. In fact, it would be a necessary response. But for a Christian to respond the same way would be an insult to God. Isaiah's response had as much to do with self-centeredness as it did with an awareness of God's holiness.

Isaiah was demonstrating the example of a man under the Law, under the Old Covenant, who realized his inadequacy and sin in the light of God's holiness. Granted, Isaiah was concerned for the state of his nation, but Isaiah was also concerned about his own standing before God in the light of his own personal sinfulness. This is the same type of response to God's presence that we saw from Adam and Eve right after the Fall.

Why would this type of response from a Christian be inappropriate? Why would it be an insult to respond in this fashion to the presence of God? Because for a New Testament Christian, Isaiah's response would completely devalue what Jesus accomplished on the cross.

Isaiah was conscious of his sin. We need to be conscious of the victory Jesus accomplished. A response of crying out, "Woe is me, I am so sinful," when we become aware of the presence of God in our life celebrates the *weakness of man and his sin*. We should be celebrating the *victory of the cross over the power of sin*.

Are there Christians who are still sinful? Yes, of course. But the sin issue—with its penalty of death—has been settled. Hebrews 9:26 says, "He then would have had to suffer often since the foundation of the world; but now, once at the end of the ages, He has appeared to put away sin by the sacrifice of Himself." In reference to the issue of sin, the writer of the letter to the Hebrews also says, "Now where there is remission of these (transgressions), there is no longer an offering for sin" (Heb. 10:18).

In other words, the sin issue has been settled, and the debt of mankind toward God has been paid by the sacrifice of Jesus, the Lamb of God. Sin stands between God and

196

man. For example, hell was never created for mankind—it was created for Satan and his demons. Sin doesn't send people to hell; unbelief does. Not choosing to believe and place our trust in what Jesus accomplished on the cross causes a person to spend eternity apart from God. The debt that sin created has been paid. The law that had been broken with its requirements has been fulfilled.

Isaiah's experience in Isaiah 6:1–2 is a moment—a brief experience of being truly overwhelmed by a revelation of the majesty of God. It was a man's moment of surrender to the lordship of a mighty God. Though others will seek to experience the same, a brief moment of a revelation of God's majesty will never be enough. We need more than just periodic moments of the revelation of God's holiness upon our lives—we need a *lifetime* of surrender and service to His lordship.

We will never discover God's power for a lifetime if we approach Him as those under the Old Covenant—a time *before* the penalty of sin had been paid for.

What should our response be to a revelation of God's power and majesty in our lives? We should definitely have an attitude of reverence. But I also believe that we should have an attitude of joy and celebration. Not a celebration of our sins and failures, but a celebration of Jesus' victory and power over sin. As New Testament Christians our response to God's presence should not be one of dread—but of hope.

The penalty of sin has been paid. There is no reason for us to have a "woe is me" attitude. Rather we should have an attitude of thanksgiving, joy, hope and surrender.

What Is the Fear of God?

Jesus summed up the entire law of God with two commands: *Love God with all of your heart, mind and strength, and love your neighbor as yourself.* The Ten Commandments can be broken down into two distinct categories: how we relate to God, and how we relate to others. Here is the point of the matter: *Our relationship with God determines our relationship with others.* In other words, the status of my relationship with God determines the status of my relationships with others. My vertical relationship determines my horizontal relationships. In Ephesians 5:21, the apostle Paul says it this way, "Submitting to one another in the fear of God."

It doesn't matter how many power encounters you have with God if you can't love your enemies. It doesn't matter how long you shook under the power of God in "fear and trembling" if you can't truly bless those who curse you. The true test of whether someone is walking in the fear of the Lord is in how they treat others. A true fear of God will translate into a genuine love for the brethren.

In 1 Thessalonians 3:12–13 the apostle Paul says:

> And may the Lord make you increase and abound in love to one another and to all, just as we do to you, so that He may establish your hearts blameless in holiness before our God and Father at the coming of our Lord Jesus Christ with all His saints.

Notice that Paul is saying that as our love for others increases, our hearts are established in holiness. We can distinguish some of the characteristics of a biblical fear of the Lord.

Patience

Love for the brethren will demonstrate itself in many ways. One way is an expression of patience. Usually when we talk about patience, it's thought of in terms that relate to our own lives. We define patience by the way it applies to things relating directly to our welfare.

We must move beyond thinking of the force of patience in terms of our own needs. Patience is emotional diligence. Many times, patience is being willing to suffer on the inside for the sake of someone else.

In 2 Timothy, the apostle Paul said something interesting about patience to the young minister Timothy. Concerning his own ministry, Paul said:

> Therefore I endure all things for the sake of the elect, that they also may obtain the salvation which is in Christ Jesus with eternal glory.
> —2 TIMOTHY 2:10

What a powerful statement! Within endurance is patience. You can't have one without the other. Paul said that he endured *all things* for the sake of the elect. I have seen preachers walk through hell, showing a tremendous amount of patience, for the sake of their ministry. I have known very few who would walk through the same hell, patiently enduring all, for the sake of someone else. The fear of God that results in love for others will empower us to do just that.

A lack of judgment toward others

In Matthew 7:1 we read, "Judge not, that you be not judged." Judgment results in passing sentence upon someone's life, imprisoning them with our opinion. Therefore, regardless of what God is able to do in their lives, our judgment blinds us from recognizing the change He made in them. But judgment doesn't begin when we notice what someone did. It begins when we are arrogant enough to think that we know *why* they did *what* they did.

As long as I refuse to give up thinking that I know why someone has behaved in a certain manner, it will be impossible for me to forgive that person. When the fear of God is a part of our lives, we will refrain from sitting on the seat of judgment, knowing that God alone is qualified for that position.

Preferring others

In Philippians 2:3–4 the apostle Paul says:

> Let nothing be done through selfish ambition or conceit, but in lowliness of mind let each esteem others better than himself. Let each of you look out not only for his own interests, but also for the interests of others.

One who has truly been captured by the fear of God will find the grace to desire to empower others above himself. It is natural to be concerned about our own interests. The prevalent thought in our society is that if I don't look out after myself, no one else will. It is true that those who are genuinely interested in your welfare may be rare. Yet true as that may be, there is One who is looking out for your best interests. Therefore, you don't need to defend or protect yourself. You can afford to extend yourself for the benefit of someone else.

The fear of God elevates the reality of God's faithfulness in our hearts, enabling us to love our neighbor as well as our enemies.

WHAT HINDERS A FEAR OF GOD

I think that one of the things that can hinder us from possessing the fear of God is familiarity. I am sure that you have heard the old saying, "Familiarity breeds contempt." This was certainly true in Jesus' case. Mark 6:2–4 records this fact, saying:

> And when the Sabbath had come, He began to teach in the synagogue. And many hearing Him were astonished, saying, "Where did this Man get these things? And what wisdom is this which is given to Him, that such mighty works are performed by His hands! Is this not the carpenter, the Son of Mary, and brother of James, Joses, Judas, and Simon? And are not His sisters here with us?" So they were offended at Him.

I find these verses fascinating. As the crowd heard Jesus teach, they recognized the wisdom with which He taught. They saw the miracles He performed. Yet they could not reconcile what they were seeing and hearing with what they knew of Jesus. He had lived among them. The people in these verses had watched Jesus grow up.

They knew his brothers and sisters. It was because they were so familiar with Jesus that it was difficult to accept Him and His teaching.

So, because they couldn't reconcile what they saw and heard with their familiarity with Jesus, they became offended at Him. There is a verse of scripture in the Gospel of Luke that might shed some additional light on why those in Jesus' own region had difficulty accepting Him. In Luke 4:22 we read:

> So all bore witness to Him, and marveled at the gracious words which proceeded out of His mouth. And they said, "Is this not Joseph's son?"

Initially, as we read that scripture it may be hard to understand what they were saying. They recognized that Jesus' words were filled with the grace of God. They were amazed the wisdom and authority with which He spoke. But notice what they asked: "Is this not Joseph's son?"

That may seem like a harmless question, but it's really not. Jesus *wasn't* Joseph's son—Jesus was conceived by the Holy Spirit. Therefore, Mary was His mother, but the Lord God was Jesus' Father.

I am sure that word got around that Mary was pregnant before she and Joseph were married. In essence what they were saying was: "How can this illegitimate son, this one born in sin, speak to us with so much wisdom and authority? How is it that He who came into this world by sin speaks to us about the things of God?"

For most of us, I don't think that familiarity breeds contempt. Instead, I think that it is more likely to breed indifference. We become so familiar with the acts of

God and with the voice of God that we become desensitized to His presence. The challenge we face, especially here in America, is the oversaturation of the gospel. We have access to the greatest churches and ministries. We have Christian television and radio, Christian books, Christian bookstores and Christian universities. We have the best of it all.

If we don't guard our hearts, we can become dull to the things of God, losing the passion of our first love. I think children who are raised in Christian homes are good examples of this dynamic. Many times when a child is raised in the things of God, that child doesn't fully appreciate the benefits of such a heritage. They have no point of reference, so it is hard for them to know how privileged they are to grow up in a healthy environment.

WHAT CULTIVATES A FEAR OF GOD?

One thing that helps to cultivate a fear of God is an attitude of thankfulness. A thankful heart helps to maintain an attitude of reverence toward the things of God. Once we lose sight of all He has done for us, we become self-centered, focusing on what we don't have instead of concentrating on what we do have. An unthankful heart makes room for an attitude of contempt toward the goodness of God. In Romans 1:21 we see this principle expressed:

> Because, although they knew God, they did not glorify Him as God, *nor were thankful,* but became futile in their thoughts, and their foolish hearts were darkened.
>
> —EMPHASIS ADDED

This scripture clearly shows the relationship between an unthankful heart and a life void of the fear of God.

Many times, Paul encouraged the Christians of his day to maintain an attitude of thankfulness regardless of their circumstances. Even in the midst of personal need, Paul encouraged the New Testament believers to maintain a thankful heart.

In Philippians 4:6 we read, "Be anxious for nothing, but in everything by prayer and supplication, *with thanksgiving*, let your requests be made known to God" (emphasis added). A thankful heart keeps our focus on God and off ourselves.

A thankful heart keeps us in the place of worship. Psalm 100:4 says, "Enter into His gates with thanksgiving, and into His courts with praise. Be thankful to Him, and bless His name." In Hebrews 13:15 we read, "Therefore by Him let us continually offer the sacrifice of praise to God, that is, the fruit of our lips, giving thanks to His name." Thanksgiving empowers true worship. It is impossible to truly worship and live a life of rebellion at the same time. To live our lives unto ourselves, we must first abandon a life of worship. Abandoning a life of worship starts when I lose sight of all for which I can be thankful.

Begin to embrace a heart of thanksgiving. Make a list of all the things for which you can be thankful. Recognize His goodness in your life. Celebrate His faithfulness—even in the face of your failures. Choose to express thanksgiving for His presence in your life. As you do, you will begin to value in a greater way the things that bring you life, as well as reject the things that steal your joy and purpose.

The Fear of God

As we have seen throughout this book, fear is a spiritual force designed to keep us in a place of defeat and torment. The symptoms of fear can be treated medically, but medicine just deals with the symptoms. Fear doesn't come from a thankful heart, but rather from a heart of self-preservation. Therefore, fear is and always will be a spiritual issue. Fear focuses on lack—what we don't have. A spirit of thankfulness focuses our hearts and minds on the value of what we do have. Consequently, a thankful heart releases the power of God's love in our lives. It is God's love that offers the ultimate cure for fear. Whether it be the fear of failure, fear of poverty or the fear of man—God's love offers deliverance and true freedom from fear. I trust that you will make His love your pursuit as you live a life without fear.

Notes

CHAPTER 1
FEAR—MAN'S FIRST ENEMY

1. Jerilyn Ross, *Triumph Over Fear: A Book of Help and Hope for People With Anxiety, Panic Attacks and Phobias* (n.p.: Bantam Books, 1994).
2. Dr. Werner U. Spitz and Dr. Russell S. Fisher, *Mediolegal Investigation of Death—Guidelines for the Application of Pathology to Crime Investigation*. Source obtained from the Internet.

CHAPTER 4
POSSESSING YOUR NEW NATURE

1. Kenneth S. Wuest, *Word Studies in the Greek New Testament*, Vol. 1 (Grand Rapids, MI: Wm. B. Eerdmans Pub. Co., 1969), 11

CHAPTER 5
BURNING THE FUSE OF ANGER

1. Nancy Gibbs, "The Littleton Massacre," *Time Magazine*, May 3, 1999, p. 20.
2. Misty Bernall, *She Said Yes* (Farmington, PA: Plough Publishing House, 1999).
3. Dr. Leon James and Dr. Diane Nahl, *Road Rage and Aggressive Driving* (n.p.: Prometheus Books, 2000).

4. Associated Press, September 11, 1999.
5. Bill McKeown, "Husband to Be Tried in Wife's Strangling," *The Gazette*, September 22, 1999.
6. Adam Cohen, "A Portrait of a Killer," *Time Magazine*, August 9, 1999.
7. Carol Tavris, *Anger: The Misunderstood Emotion* (New York: Simon and Schuster, 1989).

CHAPTER 7
THE FEAR OF FAILURE

1. Mike Fehlauer, *Finding Freedom From the Shame of the Past* (Lake Mary, FL: Creation House, 1999), 155, 157.
2. Steve Farrar, *Finishing Strong* (Sisters, OR: Multnomah Books, 1995), 4.
3. John Hagee, *Lead On* (Dallas: Word Publishing, 1988), 72.
4. Ibid.
5. *The Challenges of the Disciplined Life: Christian Reflections on Money, Sex and Power* (San Francisco: Harper and Row, 1989), 33.
6. Ibid.
7. Richard Exley, *Perils of Power* (Tulsa, OK: Honor Books, 1988).

CHAPTER 9
A HEART OF FEAR OR A HEART OF FAITH?

1. Wuest, *Word Studies in the Greek New Testament*, 91.

Notes

CHAPTER 10
A CHILD OF THE LAW OR A SON OF LOVE?

1. Bob Yandian, *The Spirit-Controlled Life* (Springdale, PA: Whitaker House, 1996).

CHAPTER 11
THE FORCE OF LOVE

1. William Barclay, *New Testament Words* (Louisville, KY: Westminster/John Knox Press, 1976), 19.

FOUNDATION
M I N I S T R I E S

*If you would like more
information about Mike and Bonnie Fehlauer
or Foundation Ministries or their products,
please contact:*

FOUNDATION
M I N I S T R I E S

P.O. Box 63659
Colorado Springs, CO 80962-3659

(719) 592-9692

E-mail: jesusfoundation@aol.com

You can experience more of God's grace & love!

Your Walk With God Can Be Even Deeper...

With *Charisma* magazine, you'll be informed and inspired by the features and stories about what the Holy Spirit is doing in the lives of believers today.

Each issue:

- Brings you exclusive world-wide reports to rejoice over.
- Keeps you informed on the latest news from a Christian perspective.
- Includes miracle-filled testimonies to build your faith.
- Gives you access to relevant teaching and exhortation from the most respected Christian leaders of our day.

Call 1-800-829-3346 for 3 FREE trial issues
Offer #AOACHB

If you like what you see, then pay the invoice of $22.97 (**saving over 51% off the cover price**) and receive 9 more issues (12 in all). Otherwise, write "cancel" on the invoice, return it, and owe nothing.

Experience the Power of Spirit-Led Living

Charisma Offer #AOACHB
P.O. Box 420234
Palm Coast, Florida 32142-0234
www.charismamag.com